Praise for *Black Sacred Rhetoric*

This commentary is much-needed both in the church and in terms of the ongoing rhetorical conversations taking place in the theological academy. Howard is entirely at ease with the basic principles and assumptions that drive Black Preaching.

Katie Geneva Cannon
Annie Scales Rogers Professor for Christian Ethics
Union Theological Seminary and
Presbyterian School of Christian Education

Black Sacred Rhetoric is an invaluable addition to the cultural history of African Americans. Gregory Howard has made an inestimable contribution to understanding the resilience of the Black faith community... As a cultural historian, I welcome this creative and seminal work...

Rev. Wyatt Tee Walker
Pastor Emeritus
Canaan Baptist Church of Christ, Harlem, N.Y.

Howard presents the linguistic expressions which have emerged out of "Black Preaching" as a theologically credible and contributing partner in the language of preaching.

Rev. Angelo V. Chatmon
Director of Church Relations
Virginia Union University

Black

Sacred

Rhetoric

To and Sister Lee
Keep taking one step
together and God will
take two

8/17/14

Black *Sacred* Rhetoric

The Theology and Testimony of Religious Folk Talk

Gregory M. Howard

With a foreword by *Wyatt Tee Walker*

BORDERSTONE PRESS, LLC

2010

First American Edition

BORDERSTONE PRESS, LLC

Gregory M. Howard

Black Sacred Rhetoric: The Theology and Testimony of Religious Folk Talk

Foreword by Wyatt Tee Walker
Edited by Roger D. Duke
Cover Design by Christopher Cook

General editor: Brian R. Mooney

Published by BorderStone Press, LLC, PO Box 1383, Mountain Home, AR 72654
Memphis, TN | Dallas, TX

www.borderstonepress.com

ISBN: 978-0-9842284-5-4

Library of Congress Control Number: 2010938353

Table of Contents

Acknowledgements

I am grateful to God for inspiring me for such a blessed purpose in my attempt to present something back unto the Universal Church in general and the Black Church in particular that has undeniably offered so much to me. I thank God for my departed and loving parents who were unapologetically black and lovers of the church. I am also deeply appreciative for my beloved Union Branch Baptist Church family and their support, as well as my first pastoral tenure at Jerusalem Baptist Church where I began to form into thought and articulate this work.

I am indebted to Pastor Angelo V. Chatmon for always encouraging me and naming the potential that he sees in me. I am thankful as well for Dr. James H. Harris, Nathan Dell, and the late Miles Jerome Jones who challenged me as a developing preacher while in seminary. I am appreciative of the support of Drs. Henry and the late Ella Mitchell for opening their home and library of knowledge to me. I wish to acknowledge Dr. Boykin Sanders, Dr. John Kinney, James E. Cook, Kurt Clark, Frederick Lamont Gooding, Monica Spencer, Kevin Smalls, Dr. Greg Heille, Dr. Katie Geneva Cannon, and countless voices within the Black Church that served as a wisdom community throughout my research efforts and for their recommendation that this commentary be made affordable to all of those who seek theological analysis of the colorful colloquial and idiomatic holy sayings of the Black Church experience. I extend sincere gratefulness to the communities of the Samuel DeWitt Proctor School of Theology at Virginia Union University and the Baptist General Convention of Virginia for granting me a venue

Black Sacred Rhetoric

to survey their constituency.

Finally, above all I thank God for my loving and always supportive wife, Margaret and my two daughters, Destiny and Holli who have been patient throughout this process. Your support has made me strong. I thank God for all who love and demand nothing less than theologically sound and congregationally relevant preaching.

Gregory M. Howard

Foreword

Black Sacred Rhetoric is an invaluable addition to the cultural history of African Americans. Gregory Howard has made an inestimable contribution to understanding the resilience of the Black faith community and its ability to cope with the vicissitudes of daily life that is tinged with pervasive and subtle racism. It is a compendium of folk wisdom that has its foundation in the faith history of a much aggrieved community that survived 244 years of the most obscene human bondage in the history of humankind and another hundred years of American-style *apartheid* which was personally and psychologically demeaning until the good Lord sent Martin Luther King and his nonviolent legions across the Deep South.

The African American citizens of the United States combined their faith in *sweet Jesus* with the folk wisdom of the community to stave off the vagaries of life's disappointments and hardships with the stoicism of *Black Sacred Rhetoric* that developed across the generations of our sojourn in this wasteland of sorrows. The selected gems of Dr. Howard's seminal work are frequently drawn from the music-sense which is the companion of the abiding folk wisdom expressed in the faith sayings that Dr. Howard culled from the experiences of those who found them useful in their daily walk. The expressions are such an integral part of our cultural history that many times they are employed in an almost casual fashion though Howard has dissected them in such a way that their profundity is unmistakable.

In this post-modern age, these expressions are an important bridge from the *Old Time Religion* age to the *hip hop* era which has a deep

Black Sacred Rhetoric

chasm. *Black Sacred Rhetoric* encompasses the faith community's collective conclusions about coping in the same way that the Spirituals do. Another feature of this volume is the commentary that accompanies the African American calendar year that is preaching fodder for the celebrations that exist across the calendar year. As a cultural historian, I welcome this creative and seminal work of Gregory Howard.

Wyatt Tee Walker
Theologian, Author & Cultural Historian
Chester, Virginia

Introduction

BLACK SACRED RHETORIC
The Theology and Testimony Of Religious Folk Talk

Chapter One, *The Lord Will Make a Way Somehow*, presents detailed accounts of a rhetorical tradition within the Black Church that contains within itself a canon of non-biblical religious utterances. It is an overview that highlights key developments in attitudes toward the preacher and the impact that his or her appropriation of these holy sayings can have on the experienced church members' appreciated and trustworthy reception of the preacher.

Chapter Two, *Religious Rhetoric from a Black Perspective*, explores the rich history of Black Preaching in America as well as the transferable oral traditions of Africa. This chapter investigates the power of communal identification as a means of persuasion in Black Preaching. The influence of Africanized rhetorical theories, practices, and the Black community's response to religious rhetoric are examined.

Chapter Three, *Excavating the Truth*, formally names fifty-five holy sayings that are frequently used in Black liturgical settings and Black Preaching specifically. This chapter captures the confirmation of this vernacular rhetoric as normal practice in Black Preaching through seven contributing African American preachers. An analysis of the findings of several surveys and qualitative studies from various communities of faith to validate the widespread recognition, reverence, and usage of non-biblical holy sayings in Black Preaching is also provided. This chapter presents detailed responses of each of the fifty-five holy sayings and claims of their sacredness as canonized truths within the Black Church.

Chapter Four, *Going Backward in order to Move Forward*, integrates personal experience, research findings, historical perspectives to Black religious rhetoric, and sound cultural and theological consideration of these sayings to present a brief and meaningful commentary of this composition of Black Sacred Rhetoric. It is formatted in lectionary style according to the Black Church calendar year.

Black Sacred Rhetoric

Chapter 1

The Lord Will Make a Way Somehow

Black Preaching is like the playing of an old Motown hit, no matter what the contemporary or popular genre is, old-school Black Preaching still moves the listener. Kirk Byron Jones in his comparative view of jazz and preaching has said that when jazz is truly swinging, the world is challenged to present a greater manifestation of joy.[1] Likewise, old-school Black Preaching that is birthed from the joy of the preacher brings joy to the listener and causes the sleeping soul to dance the way it use to dance. The rhetorical approaches and holy utterances of yesteryear that were liberating, comforting, and hopeful back then are still capable of moving the hearts and minds of modern-day listeners as well as helping to bridge the generational gap between congregants. Furthermore, old-school Black Preaching whereby both biblical and non-biblical "holy sayings" are contextualized with appropriate commentary and partnered with sound biblical hermeneutics and congregational exegesis can become the music that directs the dance between the preacher and church member.

I can recall how countless wedding receptions, birthday parties, and retirement ceremonies that included formal addresses, dinner, and dance became truly festive and how new memories were created and relationships were re-established after a rhythmic old-school jam like

---

[1] Kirk Byron Jones, *The Jazz of Preaching: How to Preach with Great Freedom and Joy* (Nashville: Abingdon Press, 2004), 125, 128.

1

Black Sacred Rhetoric

Marvin Gaye's "Got to Give it Up," Frankie Beverly's "Before I Let Go," Al Green's "Love and Happiness," or Marcia Griffiths' "Electric Slide" rang out. Noticeably, attendees of different generations collided together on the floor—dancing and relating to the same rhythm and song that reverberated love, community, and happiness. I believe that the preaching of some of our non-biblical ancestral and holy sayings that were formed from our Christian experience, with many written as spirituals or hymns, have that same effect within the dancehall of liturgical preaching. In order to become the music that compels each one to dance and become acquainted with their partner, the meaning of these holy sayings must be constructed on behalf of the listeners by the preacher.

The old-school sermonic song of Black Preaching must have contemporary relevance. As Lenora Tubbs Tisdale states, "Two things which had not previously been placed side-by-side—namely a particular biblical text (or texts) and a particular congregational context—are allowed to live together and talk together and dance with one another in the imagination of the preacher, until something new occurs through their encounter."[2] It is my contention that this imaginative dance within the preacher's mind is not only an appropriate hermeneutical approach to constructing congregational and cultural meaning of an old text, but it is what takes place when the preaching is played in the ballroom of Black sanctuaries in particular.

I have attended many church services to which I was invited as guest minister for a special occasion worship service or as the week-long revivalist. To my consternation I have often been the youngest person in attendance. Even as a thirty-plus year old preacher who was

---

[2] Leonora Tubbs Tisdale, *Preaching as Local Theology and Folk Art* (Minneapolis: Fortress Press, 1997), 38.

reared in rural Virginia, I still attend services where I am the only person less than forty years old and in some cases where I am looked upon as a child by many of the more seasoned congregants. Members in these churches seem to view younger preachers as being influenced by popular televangelistic preaching, and they assume that there is some inherent generational detachment, particularly when it comes to church matters. "What can this young fella say to us?" In response, I would simply stand to my feet and remind the church that *"God is good,"* and in response they would say, *"All the time,"* followed by my resounding affirmation, that *"All the time,"* drawing their collective response, *"God is good!"* I would make it clear that the same God that *"woke them up early this morning, clothed in their right mind, with blood still running warm through their veins"* is the same God that *"started me on my way."*

Upon displaying my knowledge and genuine appreciation of the "holy sayings" within the Black Church I felt a mutual kindred and welcoming spirit as I heard more clearly what was not being said: "Preach preacher!" We were now able to sermonically dance with one another to a familiar song while still leaving room for a re-mix or fresh word to come forth. In order for me to bring forth a convicting and culturally relevant word that would address their contemporary needs I had to enter through the door of familiarity. Samuel DeWitt Proctor wrote, "Preaching at its best will begin where the people are, and educate them in the possibilities of refined and improved human relations."[3] Preaching in a sense does not commence from the pulpit, but it rather starts in the pews. Henry H. Mitchell brought this reality to my remembrance when he stated:

---

[3] Samuel D. Proctor, *The Certain Sound of the Trumpet: Crafting a Sermon of Authority* (Valley Forge: Judson Press, 1994), 15.

> The mainstream middle class churches of today are suffering
> decline, in part because their clergy have been taught to scoff at
> and war against the "less intellectual" belief system of the average
> member.... If such clergy had only instructed the people from the
> people's own frame of reference, then the people might have gladly
> defended the pastor's right to follow his or her prophetic
> conscience.[4]

Through experiences such as this I learned that *through robust
theological and rhetorical appropriation to preaching of the holy sayings
of the Black Church experience, preachers can harness vernacular rhetoric
to enhance communal identification among African American Christians
in particular and all believing listeners in general.*[5] There is a music in
preaching that Black churches love to hear that transcends style. The
connection is not primarily made in the climatic and celebratory whoop,
tune, squall, or vivid and affecting imagery of hope in the final stages of
the sermon. I concur with Frank A. Thomas: "Celebration in the final
stage of the sermon functions as the joyful and ecstatic reinforcement of
the truth already taught and delivered in the main body of the sermon."[6]
The good news ought to joyfully lift the preacher and cause a
celebratory cry that is oftentimes expressed in stylish utterances;
however, preachers should not wait for the last sermonic song to expect
the congregation to then stand and dance with the Word of God. The

---

[4] Henry H. Mitchell, *Black Preaching: The Recovery of a Powerful Art* (Nashville: Abingdon Press, 1990), 15.

[5] My usage of "Black" is to define church, preaching, and preacher is a characterization of its Africanized liturgical style and its sociopolitical awareness and execution of liberation theology through prophetic ministry in order to bring about justice and equality for all humankind. Quotes from nineteenth and early twentieth century writers may reference "negro," "colored," or "black" as indicators of race; I however will reference African American as the people of African descent within the Black Church.

[6] Frank A. Thomas, *They Like to Never Quit Praisin' God: The Role of Celebration in Preaching* (Cleveland: Pilgrim Press, 1997), 85.

4

bond and dance between the pulpit and pew must be initiated from the beginning and throughout the preaching with theologically substantive and shared sayings as the rhythm and blues of Black Preaching.

There is some type of prophetic attractiveness for one who possesses a young face but old soul that is expressed through one's demeanor and delivery. The elocution that I am referring to is the kind that is without wordiness or the purpose of proving one's own knowledge or ability to keep it real, but which is genuine and a part of one's lived experience. In order to speak in tongues, the preacher must know the indigenous or native language, or in this case the "folk theology" of the particular community of faith.[7] Folk theology is theology that a community of people treasures and lives by that is expressed in folklore. Black Christian folklore is expressive culture that includes tales, music, dance, popular beliefs, proverbs, and oral traditions as transmitters of Black folk theology. Black Preaching is a constituent of Black folklore. I agree with Tisdale: "Preaching as folk art *(folklore)* exhibits a preference for the simple, plain, conversational speech of the local congregation."[8] This is not anti-intellectualism but a vehicle to transmit a communal belief and create a path for new ideas. To violate the folklore is to victimize the folk theology. The church knows that even an imposter can read and recite the bible as a means of persuasion, but in order to read the people one must appreciate and learn of the folklore. Many non-biblical liturgical sayings are a

---

[7] My reference of "speaking in tongue" throughout this work is an interpretation of Chapter 2 in the Acts of the Apostles wherein the Holy Spirit empowered the apostles to proclaim the Gospel in the native language (*hetero glossia*) of all that were gathered in Jerusalem on the day of Pentecost. Persons from all nations heard the apostles speaking in their own native tongues and responded to the transformative Word of God because it was presented to them in their own folk talk.

[8] Italics added for emphasis as cited in Leonora Tubbs Tisdale, *Preaching as Local Theology and Folk Art* (Minneapolis: Fortress Press, 1997), 127.

component of Black folklore, and one must know it in order to more fully communicate with the Black Church. If the preacher does not know the idiomatic religious language of the people, the preacher will not be known by the people.

Henry H. Mitchell shared with me a time when he attended a lively and fairly traditional worship experience in California. Although he did not expect to witness this southern style of Black worship in this particular township, he authentically shifted his style and diction to accommodate the congregational setting and point of reference. He did not rob or cheat the Gospel, but he made a rhetorical adjustment whereby he shared with me, "Henry whooped that day."[9]

I attended a revival service in Richmond several years ago at a church that has a prophetically charged and gifted pastor/preacher who is known for inviting high caliber preachers who can both "holla" and help somebody. At this revival, I witnessed a master of Black Sacred Rhetoric. This particular revivalist introduced himself in song and closed the service out in song, and somewhere in between that mini-concert there was a sermon. Once he approached the sacred desk he read from the scripture, prayed a prayer, and preached the Word that was accompanied with an abundance of these extra-biblical holy sayings that I call *Black Sacred Rhetoric*. The church was edified as both young and old packed the house each night and stood to their feet as a hopeful and convicting word cut them like a two-edged sword. This response was unlike any other response I had witnessed at this particular church that is known for having great revivalists and a prince of preaching as pastor. It was at that moment that I determined how Black Sacred

---

[9] This is a statement from an interview that I conducted with Dr. Henry H. Mitchell at his home in Atlanta, Georgia on July 20, 2007. Interview questions are posted in the Appendix and several responses have been interwoven within the overall text.

Rhetoric and its exegetical appropriation could cause the people of God to dance with joy, leave informed, and be convinced that a change needed to be made in their lives.

This preacher was in line with both Cicero's and Augustine's view on the role of eloquence and rhetoric.[10] This preacher touched all bases as he instructed, persuaded, and delighted the listening congregation. This phenomenon now had credible practitioners and a community of people outside of the rural setting that longed to be reminded, *"Everything that looks good to you, ain't necessarily good for you,"* and, *"If you take one step, God will take two."* This old-school Black preaching was refreshing to a contemporary "what's hot on the pop chart" society.

I must admit however that the employment of this religious vernacular has been a thorn in my flesh. Although I see its significance as a means of communal association as well as a passing on of a particular folk theology, it pains me to see the mishandling and abuse of such sacred sayings. Some preachers use these "holy sayings" or what others call "holy clichés" as artificial signals. These holy sayings are unfortunately misappropriated in order to gain an emotional response from the people of God which in return arouses the preacher's narcissistic appetite and feeds his or her plea for public affirmation. This in my view is the pseudo-prophetic prostitution of our sacred vernacular rhetoric, a rhetoric which in fact warrants and deserves to be reverently handled.

I have also witnessed what I considered to be ill-prepared sermons whereby the preacher reaches into his or her bag of "grandma

---

[10] Saint Augustine referenced Cicero's *Oration*, noting that the eloquent should speak in such a way as to instruct, delight, and move their listeners. Augustine's use of the word instruct is an interpretation of Cicero's meaning to 'prove' or 'demonstrate' as cited in *Saint Augustine On Christian Teaching*, trans. R. P. H. Green (Oxford: Oxford University Press, 1997), 117.

theology," or what Henry H. Mitchell referred to me in the aforementioned interview as "Aunt Jane's theology," and tries his or her best to salvage the sermon by declaring that *"He may not come when you want Him to, but He's always right on time! Can I get a witness? That He will pick you up, tuuurrrn you around and place your feet on much higher ground. Can I get a witness that He's an on time God? Ain't He alright? He's alright I tell you. Ain't He alright, ain't He alright!"* My response is quite simply, "Yes, God is alright, and God will indeed totally transform our lives," but where's the theological and rhetorical connectivity to the sermon's primary proposition? The lack of context to these holy sayings leads to the bastardization of this rich ancestral language.

Sunday mornings change, but the Black Church's expectation of preaching still fastens to the hope that the preacher will utter words of godly assurance during his or her sermonic exposition. Some type of biblical or extra-biblical "holy saying" that has stood the test of time is longed for and critical in order to maintain congregational attentiveness and communal identification between pew and pulpit. As believing listeners, we come with great expectation that a word will be offered that will pierce our hearts and provide hope for those of us wrestling with life's uncertainties. *"Can I get a witness that the Lord will make a way somehow?"* These tenured holy sayings, many whose birthdates are known because of their hymnal origin and others whose original source is unknown, have yet to go out of style and still provide dance line music within the context of Black Preaching. These old-school sayings can still cause us to dance with the Spirit and one another during liturgical preaching as they reinforce our faith by stating the comforting and hopeful reality that *"trouble don't last always."*

No matter how informed and eloquent a preacher's oration may be, the preacher's speech is still flawed when it endeavors to name divinity.

This flawed speech, mostly metaphoric, is nevertheless valued within practicing communities of faith because of the communities' reverent attempt to meet the challenge of expressing the glory of God or a God act as interpreted through their lived experience. Gail Ramshaw suggests that language about God (liturgical speech) must be metaphoric as it functions within a creative tradition to symbolize our faith. This metaphoric language possesses a "yes-no-yes" tension that affirms its usage because of the sacred words, rejects it because they cannot contain divinity or convey the essential being of God, and finally in return re-affirms the sacred word because it is the language of faith and our tradition of grace.[11] Brian K. Blount reminds the preacher of this truth when he states, "The preacher must not only, in a broad sense, speak the language of the listeners, but must also, in a more specific sense, use that language according to the particular linguistic prescriptions...of the cultural or sub-cultural group with whom he or she is conversing."[12] Folk theology in the form of liturgical preaching is therefore substantially expressed in the "faith talk" of vernacular rhetoric, whereby the essence of the gospel is reinterpreted and communicated through and in consideration of a people's cultural experience.

Within the Black Church, there are unique metaphorical and illustrative utterances that appropriately display a particular people's recognition and reverence of God. Moreover, there are certain dialogical and liturgical utterances such as *"He's a Bridge over troubled waters,"* *"He's a prop on every side,"* and *"There is a bright side somewhere"* that are consistently used in Black Folk Preaching. The historicity and

---

[11] Gail Ramshaw, *Reviving Sacred Speech: The Meaning of Liturgical Language* (Akron: OSL Publications, 2000), 9, 32.

[12] Brian K. Blount, *Cultural Interpretation: Reorienting New Testament Criticism* (Minneapolis: Fortress Press, 1995), 71-72.

theological gravity of these idioms form the components of what I consider to be a para-canon within the Black Church which I further classify as Black Sacred Rhetoric in Folk Preaching.[13]

Although Black Sacred Rhetoric may be heard around the house or on the street corner, this call-and-response religious speech has great liturgical value in the Black Church worship experience as made evident in its permanence. According to James F. White, this longevity is the only criterion of how significant liturgical language is to a particular community of faith.[14] Spoken both within the context of worship and in non-liturgical settings, Black Sacred Rhetoric more frequently centers upon worship and more specifically, preaching.

This language helps shape the faith of the Black Church and serves as a means of communal identification between the preacher and experienced pew. This vernacular's relevance is however being threatened with extinction due to the aforementioned prostitution and bastardization of this ancestral language as well as its tradeoff for more contemporary idioms that are being used by popular preachers who seem to believe that modern-day sayings have more appeal to a post-modern and pop-culture influenced world.

Firstly, the prostitution of Black Sacred Rhetoric is evident when it is intentionally used for entertainment and amusement, as the preacher abuses these rhetorical texts primarily for a verbal response from the parishioner. This verbal response appeases some preachers' appetite

---

[13] Boykin Sanders, professor of New Testament and Greek Studies at the Samuel DeWitt Proctor School of Theology at Virginia Union University and former pastor of Dexter Avenue King Memorial Baptist Church (1990-1991) in Montgomery, Alabama declaratively suggested to me: "This Black Sacred Rhetoric is in fact canon unto the Black Church". Sanders' view of canon is that which is accepted as truths and practiced within the dynamics of liturgy and religious traditions.

[14] James F. White, "The Study of Protestant Worship," in *Protestant Worship: Traditions in Transition*, (Louisville: Westminster/John Knox Press, 1989), 15.

for both public and instant affirmation while preaching. The preacher is a complex being in that the preacher assumes the position of being used as an instrument to communicate God's will to the people of God. However, as finite and flesh-draped creations, preachers still long for evidence that their effort has not hindered the Word of God from moving upon the hearts of humankind.

This hidden intentionality to be heard and understood as opposed to primarily being applauded resonates within the soul of preachers. The risk therefore becomes greater of using vernacular rhetoric as a means to make the folk shout or declare unto the preacher "say it preacher" or "you are talking now" in order to validate his or her voice while preaching. To the chagrin of the legacy and value of these holy sayings, they are cheapened as they are objectified for the purpose of emotionalism or as crowd pleasers. When prostituted in this fashion, these expressions loose authentic liturgical value.

Secondly, the bastardization of Black Sacred Rhetoric is apparent when these holy idioms are spoken without meaning, context, or commentary. These idioms' true essence and interpretative meaning are oftentimes aborted and left to stand alone as they are subjugated to the low status of sermonic fillers instead of being sermonic supporters or illustrative oral imagery. Black Sacred Rhetoric is not an orphan vernacular but was birthed through hymns and the believers' interpretation of the splendor and movement of God in their lives. The bastardization of this liturgical dialect takes form when the preacher declares that *"He's been better to me than I've been to myself"* without expounding upon how this is so.

The preacher must become a mediator of meaning not only for the presentation of particular biblical texts but also for other happenings of grace, for liturgical expressions and gestures, and certainly for Black

Sacred Rhetoric. Much like David Buttrick's concern with the "biblical" preaching tradition and its purpose to tell the biblical story, but at the cost of preachers who oftentimes fail to name God-with-us in the world, we can bastardize Black Sacred Rhetoric by not wedding it to appropriate commentary and to congregational implications which support its usage.[15]

The people of God deserve to know what it means when a preacher proclaims, *"Everyday will be like Sunday, and Sabbath will have no end."* To echo Robert Waznak, meaning and the surplus thereof must be made available to the listener of these holy sayings. The preacher as mediator of meaning does not teach the congregant what he or she already knows, but the preacher provides a deeper and more relevant meaning of the phenomena (holy sayings).[16] Mary Catherine Hilkert in *Naming Grace* determined, "Preaching requires the contemplative and prophetic gifts of making connections between the story of God's fidelity in the past, God's continuing fidelity in the present, and God's promise of a future full of hope."[17] This requires interpretation of the old sayings in order to forge fresh and relevant meaning. The old should not be abandoned and buried but should be made real through appropriate commentary and the exegesis of a particular text and congregational context.

Thirdly, longstanding and theologically substantive statements are being sacrificed in the tradeoff. The tradeoff of Black Sacred liturgical rhetoric for exclusively contemporary sayings widens the generational

---

[15] David Buttrick, *Homiletic: Moves and Structures* (Philadelphia: Fortress Press, 1987), 17.

[16] Robert P. Waznak, *An Introduction to the Homily* (Collegeville: Liturgical Press, 1998), 14.

[17] Mary Catherine Hilkert, *Naming Grace: Preaching and the Sacramental Imagination* (New York: Continuum, 1997), 56.

chasm within the Black Church. This gap is most noticeable between the experienced church member and the new pastor or the experienced church members and the more contemporary Generation X church member. Unfortunately, this liturgical and generational bifurcation potentially breeds distrust between the younger preacher and those who value Black Sacred Rhetoric. A friend shared with me that after preaching a fervent word, an elderly stateswoman of the church approached him and communicated with him that she was so glad that he spoke from their point of reference. In his view there was a homiletical suspicion and tiredness within the church of hearing what so many others consider to be popular "street talk" converted into holy clichés as a means to awaken the crowd.

This line of argument is not a homiletical grievance against those who make an effort to reach today's youngsters or those who are proud patrons of the Hip Hop culture by interpreting and communicating the Gospel in partnership with today's popular sayings. I am a proponent for the usage of contemporary rhetorical and homiletical theories as a means to speak in tongue. The Apostle Paul so eloquently reminded us of the deliberate pluralist approach of preaching for the sake of spreading the Gospel when he said unto the Church in Corinth: "And unto the Jew I became as a Jew, that I might gain the Jews...; to them that are without law, I became as one without law, being not without law to God but under law to Christ, that I might gain them that are without law" (I Corinthians 9: 19-23). Andrew Carl Wisdom, much like others in the Black Church, has noted that boredom in the pews is related primarily to preaching which lacks a congregational, cultural, or generational connection. This poor interpretation and rhetorical presentation of the issues and symbols that both the old and young of this "generationally historic" moment are left to carry as baggage, in the midst of an irrelevant faith, must lend itself to a new vernacular. Preaching must not fail to address the hub symbols and symbolic activism of each particular generation.[18]

I support this attempt to name grace in terms of the faith experience of a community or culture of people, knowing that doing so involves listening, learning from, and speaking in the tongue of the community— as in the case of the so-called Hip-Hop Generation. Nevertheless, let us not lose sight of Black Sacred Rhetoric's ability to still make people of faith dance. Sound Black preaching must challenge those who intentionally or unknowingly misuse Black Sacred Rhetoric, or worse yet bury this vernacular in the catacombs of so-called "old time religion."

Old-time religion, with its organizational structures, conservative worship, dogmatic doctrines, and androcentric denominational traditions, can be looked upon as being exclusive, oppressive, and subsequently irrelevant to today's world. Black Sacred Rhetoric is neither old-time religion nor either/or religious rhetoric, but rather it is a para-canon unto the Black Church that speaks of an anamnetic and doxological glorification of God for those in need of an affirming, informing, or hopeful word. Although many of these sayings are in a masculine voice, I believe that they are inherently inclusive and liberating, as the theology is vested in the grace and movement of God rather than God's gender or ethnic biases. The cheapening and misusage of these holy proverbs require a balance in the trading off of vernacular rhetoric in order to reach a particular faith group.

The tradeoff is tolerable but requires perspective. In a world of pluralism and symbolism where Joseph Webb raised the question "Why

---

[18] Andrew Carl Wisdom, *Preaching to a Multi-Generational Assembly* (Collegeville: Liturgical Press, 2004), 7, 73.

We See Things Differently?", the preacher must learn of a multiplicity of rhetorical theories and approaches; otherwise, young people in particular will forever be in the search of less familiar voices to help frame new definitions of their crumbling symbols.[19] This is the case as well for the more experienced church member who longs for but has yet to be taken back to the place where he or she first believed. Black Sacred Rhetoric and other ecclesial traditions are hub symbols (core values) to many believers, and the pluralist preacher must maintain a high degree of integrity when employing them. Joseph Webb stresses the nature of pluralist integrity in the following statement:

> Pluralistic integrity requires an awareness that what we have called hub symbols are at the core of every one of us—they are symbols that are "sacred." ...Pluralistic integrity requires each one of us to develop as full an understanding as possible of what our own hub symbols actually are.... Pluralistic integrity also requires an awareness of what is going on in another person when he or she erupts with anger, defensiveness, or hostility.... A hub symbol of some kind has been seriously challenged, even wounded.[20]

The hub symbols of both the newly forging generation and the more tenured and traditionalist-type church member must be honored and made a part of the preaching experience. Just as the preacher adopts certain street language as a means of identifying with Generation X or the Hip Hop culture, Black Sacred Rhetoric is a means of communal identification within the experienced Black Church. I admittedly celebrate and regularly employ the hermeneutical lenses and homiletical approaches that are superbly used by the likes of Otis Moss

---

[19] Joseph M. Webb, *Preaching and the Challenge of Pluralism* (St. Louis: Chalice Press, 1998), 36.
[20] Ibid., 58-60.

III, Kevin Smalls, Frederick L. Gooding, and others of the *Gospel Remix* genre of preaching, as a vehicle to attract a Gospel-seeking audience that is currently culturally influenced by Hip Hop—just as it was the case during the Bee Bop, Pop, Disco, and "Say it Loud I'm Black and I'm Proud" era. I am yet still advocating for Black Sacred Rhetoric's just due and proper place within Black liturgy and Black preaching, as a treasure and means of communal recognition, as is Hip Hop is to others.[21]

Henry H. Mitchell suggests that hearers welcome wisdom and newness as long as they are extensions of the faith already accepted. Mitchell also noted in *Black Preaching: The Recovery of a Powerful Art* that acculturated speech helps to avoid making the hearers feel that their ancestral wisdom and identity are under attack.[22] Once again, this is not a grievance against the use of modern day culturally sensitive techniques, sayings, and approaches to reach today's Generational X or Hip Hop culture. Rather, it is an attempt to keep Black Sacred Rhetoric alive and available to those who treasure it but may be malnourished due to it having been taken off of some homiletical shelves or served without properly preparing it.

The preacher's strict and sole allegiance to contemporary rhetoric in order to captivate the contemporary culture blesses some, just as relevant illustrations help present the Gospel in a twenty-first century form. Exclusive use of these forms, however, runs the risks of flooding the church with shadow energy. Unfortunately, in a developing tendency, preachers depreciate our post-Africa ancestral religious

---

[21] The "Gospel Remix" genre of preaching inferences the art of preaching within today's Hip Hop culture in a way that creatively communicates the relevancy of the Gospel. Ralph C. Watkins captures several pastors' perspectives that masterfully preach and teach in this genre in *Gospel Remix: Reaching the Hip Hop Generation* (Judson Press, 2007).

[22] Henry H. Mitchell, *Black Preaching: The Recovery of a Powerful Art* (Nashville: Abingdon Press, 1990), 15.

language, and tenured believers become disengaged from the liturgical experience. Some African American preachers have taken significant ancestral religious rhetoric for granted and have allowed it to go out of style by forcing contemporary idioms upon Black traditional churches in order to attract today's believer. In our effort to "keep it real" and hold the interest of younger members, we have ignored how traditional folk theology gains the support of the mature congregant.

A homiletical colleague and dear friend of mine shared with me a noteworthy preaching experience he had while being considered for the pastoral position at a prominent and progressive Baptist church in Alabama. At the time he was one of three finalists, and after an extensive interview process it was his opportunity to stand behind the sacred desk before the people of God. The two other candidates, both learned men of God in their mid-thirties to early forties, had preached the two preceding Sundays. My friend preached that day, not as one who was a candidate or craving for a few affirming amens, but as pastor. That is to say he preached as though he knew the people. He did not dance around the reality of both personal and communal pain, moments of silence and isolation, and the uncertainties and thorns of life. With total humility and still awestricken with how God used him, he told me that he felt as if he had assisted in the reclamation and renaissance of the Black Baptist pulpit that day by standing flatfooted and as tall as his five-foot eight body could stand and proclaiming the Word of God in the people's native tongue. He appropriately interjected and made applicable the dialogical and liturgical utterances from the Black Church's para-canon that I have classified as Black Sacred Rhetoric. He believed that he was able to connect with the people; both the young and restless and those who have been watching the world turn for quite some time.

After preaching, my friend said that he came down from behind the lectern, demounted the pulpit, and greeted as many as he could as a sea of multi-generational persons complimented him and praised God for the Word. One well-kept and vibrant mother of the church who seemed to be in her late seventies approached him with a stare of admiration and approval as she reached up to tell him, "I'm so glad that you didn't stand up there and say what all these other preachers are now saying. Our prayers have been answered, and I hope to hear from you again real soon, Pastor." Two weeks later my friend was called to pastor that church. My friend, who was thirty-five years old and young in face at the time, realized that Black Sacred Rhetoric appropriately presented as old-school preaching caused all of the people to dance that day. The preaching was made plain and relevant without telling everyone to "drop it like it's hot," and because he told the story and offered ways whereby God will make a way. He did not have to tell the church the spiritually deflating and self-evident axiom, "O, you just missed it; you'll catch it on your way home." The truth was revealed, and they got it that day as they were reminded, *"Everything that looks or for that matter sounds good to you is not necessarily good for you."*

I applaud my preacher friend for valiantly defending and reverently handling Black Sacred Rhetoric as a constituent of sound and relevant preaching. However, in order to treat some preachers' addiction to shaping liturgy according to an ever-changing popular culture, in order to maintain consistent liturgical expressions, in order to rebuild the communicative breakdown between preacher and experienced church member, and in order to save sacred linguistic traditions, an authentic and authoritative stance must be taken to secure Black Sacred Rhetoric.

Black Sacred Rhetoric can be presented in a structured and calendrical system for the purpose of concretizing it within the context of liturgical preaching and preventing its extinction, insuring its legacy, and promoting its deployment without exploitation. Violation of one's frame of reference or ancestral wisdom can be suicidal to a preacher's attempt to establish a rapport and trust with the congregation, especially when he or she is already skating on the thin ice of a Word Network and TBN influenced perception of today's preacher.

I was blessed on one occasion with the opportunity to preach to the Division of Clergy at an annual state convention. My heart and head counted the honored occasion as a privilege and a priceless learning experience, while my nerves considered the exposure to be a quasi-Golgotha. Nevertheless, after much prayer and hours within the homiletical city of preparation, I packed my preaching bags, headed to that mountain of a hotel and conference center, and eventually harnessed the make-shift pulpit while being flanked by giants of our Faith. I was being microscopically examined by friends, mentors, former professors, a sea of unfamiliar faces, and a guest homiletical lecturer, author, and professor of a reputable seminary.

My point of departure was from Exodus 3, and my sermon title was from within the text: *This is Holy Ground* (See Appendix A). I was led to assert that post modernity is a great gift as we are privileged to question and examine that which has been identified by a few as the totality of truth. Yet, still there are some things that were created by God with the intent to remain holy and unlike the new.

The sermon's celebratory close referenced the word of God that was spoken to Moses through the burning bush for the purposes of assuring, comforting, informing, and making hopeful the Israelites who were currently being enslaved by the suzerain nation of Egypt.[23] This once

---

[23] This sermon asserted that the Word of God that was given to Moses was in a vernacular rhetoric uniquely identifiable among the oppressed and the oppressors. This word was inscribed in stone as the law. This word was however proclaimed and solidified as part of an oral folk-lore that expressed a folk belief that God the Deliverer is on the side of the oppressed.

bashful, boney, and bucktoothed little boy from the backwoods of Virginia reminded every listener of that vernacular rhetoric from within the burning bush of the Black Church experience and para-canon—*"we shall overcome!"* The art of anaphora was used to begin each successive clause with, "street talk says...but God talk says *The Lord will make a way somehow!"* Those who were in attendance, both learned and unlearned, from the rural settings and cities throughout the state, silk stocking church leaders and storefront church pastors, acknowledged to me the need to continue to preach from the past to the present, so that the richness and valuable assets of our past will not be forgotten.

A connection was made and I was invited to the table whereby the rest of who I am and what I have to offer was afforded a voice and subsequent support, now that I was able to identify with the mothers and fathers of the faith. This is not a sell-out for me; it is who I am and the liturgical language that I was raised by. Like love, it does not require or ask of anything in return. Button-pushers are quick fixes that grope for a quick emotional response, but Black Sacred Rhetoric is anamnetic in that it memorializes a God act and epikletic in that it invokes worship of God and a sense of togetherness and identity among the believers. The use of this vernacular in order to connect with God's people so that God's kingdom building plan can go forth and the rest of one's voice can be heard is not sycophancy. The preacher should never become a slave of popular culture in order to win the favor of even a few thousand by flattering persons of influence so that he or she can advance him or herself.

Incorporating Black Sacred Rhetoric into preaching is an honoring of a forgotten generation and of a community of faith that needs to hear what mama used to faithfully mumble and spiritually dance to, just as the Hip Hop culture needs to hear "It's getting hot in here!" when trying to bring fashionable relevance to the burning bush or three Hebrew boys texts. Contemporary culture is forever advancing a new and faddish reality, and with each new cultural turn comes new witnesses and words that can be partnered in our preaching effort. However, to prevent the communal chasm among the saints and the burial of yet another Black tradition within the Black Church, African American preachers need to make room for these holy sayings of the Black Church experience. A residence must be established for this cherished liturgical language. Otherwise, the winds and foul weather of popular preaching will blow it away like a lifeless leaf.

Chapter 2

Religious Rhetoric from a Black Perspective

Man in Africa, as elsewhere, has sought to relate his past
to his present, and to tentatively explore the future so that
he might not stand lonely and isolated in the great sweep
of time, or intimidated by the formidable earth and the
vast stretch of surrounding seas.[24]

—Harold Courlander

Does history have a beginning or permanent place of residency? The pursuit to catalogue and name what has already happened is a laborious and continuous process of unearthing shaded facts that predate the researcher's presumptions of a particular matter. The roots of history are sometimes hard to find within the deep soils of centuries past. Nevertheless, in order to give credence and perspective to developing ideas one must examine the hollowed walls of a familiar but yet disjointed past to uncover related or supportive evidence for newly named phenomena. Discovering the history of Black Sacred Rhetoric, and more specifically Black Preaching, is no exception.

Although Black Christian Preaching is American, its essence and style were conceived on the continent of Africa. Much like the automobiles manufactured in American Toyota and Honda plants but

---

[24] Harold Courlander, *A Treasury of African Folklore* (New York: Marlowe and company, 1996), 1.

envisioned in Japan, the Blackness witnessed in American Christian Preaching was born here but conceived in Africa.

The blackness of Christian Preaching is, in fact, African. The stylish and rhetorical hue of Black Preaching was not founded in Colonial America but first fostered in the ancestral lives of an African people. As Henry H. Mitchell has stated, "African religions have neither founders nor reformers. They have neither 'authorized versions' nor canonical scriptures... Religions simply flow out of the life of the peoples."[25] Harold Courlander's exploration of African Folklore brought him to a similar resolve:

> The myths, legends, epics, tales, historical poems and countless other traditional oral literary forms [religious rhetoric] of African peoples have been woven out of the substance of human experience: struggles with the land and the elements, movements and migrations, wars between kingdoms, conflicts over pastures and waterholes, and wrestlings with mysteries of existence, life and death.[26]

History rests somewhere between an actual event, the results thereof, and a particular people's interpretation. Thusly, identifying the precise place of origin and naming Black Preaching's African mother and father and its subsequent American foster-parent is virtually impossible. Sketches of its essence are conversely evident in its juxtaposition to Western African religious traditions. Many religious

---

[25] Henry H. Mitchell, *Black Belief: Folk Beliefs of Blacks in America and West Africa* (New York: Harper and Row, 1975), 61.

[26] Courlander examined countless people and traditions in Africa and their oral literature, traditions, myths, legends, epics, tales, recollections, wisdom, and sayings in an attempt to properly classify and celebrate the myriad of African folklore. He further cautioned the widespread characterization of all African societies and cultures as "African" or "the African experience" as cited in Harold Courlander, *A Treasury of African Folklore* (New York: Marlowe and Company, 1996), 1.

traditions, stories, and oral practices of the Akan people, such as the Asante Nation in particular and even the Fante people of the Cape Coast, reflective in today's Black Church experience.[27]

Coming to America: African Religious Traditions in America

Although the arrival of America's first African slaves is easily traced to 1619, the duration of the trans-Atlantic slave trade complicates the pursuit to associate the African Americans' Christian experience to particular African providences. Countless slaves came from a myriad of tribes, nations, and language groups stretching the entire African coastline. The largest percentile of American slaves was imported from West Africa and the Congo-Angola region.[28] The multicultural and pluralistic religious traditions of Africa make religious society unique; however, the vast majority is joined in similar core beliefs, such as the belief in a supreme Creator of heaven and earth and ritualistic expressions of faith through dancing, drumming, and singing.[29] Moreover, the religious languages and speech of Africa are tonal, practically illustrative, and contextually relevant. Henry H. Mitchell adds:

> At no point did the African rhetorical tradition permit emphasis on abstractness.... The Yorubas of Nigeria [for instance] insist that ideas be expressed in images common people can visualize.... The African insistence on images and action, tales and pictures with

---

[27] This is anecdotal observation that occurred to me while on a mission trip in Ghana from June 1, 2010 to June 28, 2010.

[28] Albert J. Raboteau, *Slave Religion: The "Invisible Institution" in the Antebellum South* (Oxford: Oxford University Press, 1978), 7.

[29] Ibid., 15.

meaning, is no figment of a primitive imagination: It is a sophisticated principle of communication.[30]

African religious traditions cannot be singularized, for they have countless theological and anthropological variations. Estimates range around three thousand of the African Traditional Religions (ATR), which are based upon individual tribes or peoples; they are not homogenous but yet have commonalities.[31] The religion of the African is so deeply rooted in his or her being that persons cannot separate themselves from their religion, for to do so would equate to severing ties with their family and roots. ATR consider God, natural phenomena, and one's ancestors to be intrinsically related to one another for the purpose of benefiting humanity. They are primarily monotheistic but operationally polytheistic as well as practical as opposed to philosophical. These religious practices are distinct as well because there is no demarcation between that which is secular and sacred or religious and non-religious.[32] The axioms and language of African religious traditionalists are expressed in all places, just as Black Sacred Rhetoric is witnessed both in religious community and around the kitchen. Another commonality among ATR is that they are deeply expressive, through dance, instrument, and story vis-à-vis proverb. The eighteenth century Nigerian-born freed American slave Olaudah Equiano, candidly wrote that after learning to read and his exploration of the stories of the Bible, he surprisingly discovered within the Judeo-Christian story "the laws

---

[30] Henry H. Mitchell, *Black Preaching: The Recovery of a Powerful Art* (Nashville: Abingdon, 1990), 31.

[31] Henceforth in this volume African Traditional Religions will be represented by ATR. This is a term that is used by some historians, theologians, socialists, and cultural anthropologists.

[32] John S Mbiti, *African Religions and Philosophy: 2nd Edition* (New Hampshire: Heinemann, 1990), 2.

and rules of my own country written almost exactly."[33] This purports the assumption that there are ritualistic congruencies even between some African Traditional Religions and Christianity. Furthermore, some historians have not only catalogued the religious and cultural similarities between the Akan people of today and the biblical Israelites, but J.B. Dankwa and Osei Kwadwo have even suggested that they are of the same mixed stock and shared in boundary communities within the ancient Mesopotamian world before migrating to Africa.[34]

Doctrines and views on God and creation can be forever juxtaposed and debated for the purpose of comparing historical facts and today's global significance. African religious traditions' similarities in rhetorical form, ritual, and worship can however be useful for investigating the roots of the African American Christian experience and more specifically Black preaching. African religious traditions show similarities in liturgical expressions. The early seventeenth century importation of slaves brought with it African religious traditions and an inherent orality that is strikingly tonal in expressing its folklore. Proverbs were used in West Africa to pass on a worldview that may or may not have been religiously subjective. The oral tradition of the Yoruba and Ashanti nations that shaped itself into folk wisdom has greatly influenced Black culture in the Western Hemisphere.[35] Much like Negro spirituals,

---

[33] Milton C. Sernett presents a first-hand sketchy account of the Ibo religious culture as experienced and written by Olaudah Equiano. Equiano who was born in Nigeria, kidnapped at eleven, sold into American slavery, baptized as Gustavus Vassa into the Christian faith, and eventually purchased his freedom in 1766, learned how to read the Bible, and went on to establish himself with Christian abolitionists in England, whereby he spoke out against slavery throughout England as cited in Olaudah Equiano, "Traditional Ibo Religion and Culture," in *African American Religious History: A Documentary Witness*, ed. Milton C. Sernett (Durham: Duke University Press, 1999), 13.

[34] Osei Kwadwo, *An Outline of Asante History: Part 1, 3ʳᵈ Edition* (Kumasi: Cita Press, 2004), 1, 131.

[35] Henry H. Mitchell, *Black Belief: Folk Beliefs of Blacks in America and West*

Mitchell noted how folk wisdom or faith as proverb has no authorized version or beginning and therefore lends itself to a variety of interpretations on one end of the spectrum but solidifies itself as being an echoing constituent and/or background player in the Black Westerner's experience on the other end.

The assimilation and influence of African religious practices and speech into American Christianity was an inevitable effect of slave-induced pluralism. The ramifications of slavery were ethnic, religious, and cultural syncretism. ATR is still a part of the African slaves' religious life while in American bondage. O.C. Edwards, as others, noted that it was not until sometime after the second decade of the nineteenth century that the majority of African American slaves were converted to Christianity. The evangelization successes of the Second Great Awakening presented Christian preaching in an orally and culturally appetizing way that was common to ATR.[36] The practices of many African religious traditions were still being kept and practiced alongside Christianity in the countless hush harbors and secret worship services of the night. African American slaves preferred their secluded worship services over the White Christian church experience because they had the freedom to pray, dance, sing, and exhort in their own vernacular rhetoric—a vernacular that was expressive of their vivid memory of African religious customs.[37]

Although some slaves and their fore-parents may have been introduced to Christianity as early as the 1400s through missionaries throughout West Africa, Christianity was foreign to the majority of African American slaves. African American slaves did find familiarity in

---

Africa (New York: Harper and Row, 1975), 63-64.

[36] O.C. Edwards Jr., *A History of Preaching* (Nashville: Abingdon Press, 2004), 529.

[37] Albert J. Raboteau, *Slave Religion: The Invisible Institution in the Antebellum South* (Oxford: Oxford University Press, 1978), 215-216.

the rhetorical sound and the theme of deliverance in some Christian preaching. The soulfulness of Black preaching predates conversion. Soulfulness is the deeply authentic, expressive, rhythmic, and spirited nature of preaching. Soulfulness is obviously subject to imitation, but comes effortlessly to those of African descent who have unconscious memories of a richly and religiously expressive past. The method of Black Preaching came before the specific message of Christianity, for it is a constituent of the oral folklore of many African religious traditions.

Christianity on African Soil

Just as African Traditional Religions were filtered through the channels of slavery, as remnants of many of its practices and precepts were brought to America, so was Christianity brought to Africa. Although Christianity and the cradle of humanity are indigenous to East Africa, it has been well documented that Euro-American Christian preaching was introduced to many West African nations by the Portuguese missionaries of the early sixteenth century. The nations of Guinea and Kongo were of the first to have credible conversions. Nzinga Mebemba, Kongo's premier king, was converted to Christianity during his reign of 1506-1543.[38]

Throughout the late eighteenth century, Christianity established a legitimate presence throughout West African provinces through the return and ministry of Americanized slaves. Conversely, Christianity may had been informally presented to many African slaves and traditional religionists who were among the Pre-Americas' slave trade

---

[38] Albert J. Raboteau, *Slave Religion: The* "The Invisible Institution" *in the Antebellum South* (Oxford: Oxford University Press, 1978), 6.

of the 1400s and subsequent centuries. Albert J. Raboteau further recorded that as a prologue to the Atlantic slave trade, the Portuguese were capturing West African light-skinned Berbers in the 1440s. Whether it is conjecture or historical probability, the Portuguese's nationalistic movement into Africa and their subsequent evangelization efforts that extended well into the 1500s, may have actually planted seeds of Christianity one century earlier.

The whipping of slaves into Christianized submission and the slaves' eventual mastering of the Christian faith were a bicoastal reality. Christian conversion in both America and West Africa was a consequence to the adaptation of an instinctively religious African people whose former religion was not totally intact due to a separation from homeland soil, surroundings, symbols, personal freedom, and kindred. Christianity had a small presence in Africa as it even made its way inland before the Atlantic slave trade. However, in spite of the king of Kongo's sixteenth century conversion as well as other tribal leaders and their presumable influence over those they lead, Christian missionaries had little success prior to the European colonization efforts of the nineteenth century. Whispers of Christianity may have been heard by African slaves, but as Raboteau stated: "By far the greatest number of those Africans who fell victim to the Atlantic slave trade came from peoples who held the indigenous and traditional beliefs of their fathers."[39] Many African slaves kept the roots of their African religious traditions watered by gathering in secret, in both enslaved Africa and the Americas.

---

[39] Ibid., 7.

A Child is Born: Black Preaching

Through secret prayer and worship meetings, Africans in America were able to keep some of their traditions on life support until their conversion to Christianity and the subsequent emergence of Black congregations during the 1770s and 1780s.[40] The slaves mastering of their masters' faith invoked an untold awakening in American religious history. African-Americans became more Christian than whites as "they were confirmed in the knowledge of their own moral superiority and further strengthened in their claim to ultimate vindication."[41] Christianity became to African Americans what whites had not intended. Enslaved African-Americans discovered theological evidence that God was on the side of the oppressed and the liturgical expressions, gestures, and rituals that mirrored their African roots. Gayraud S. Wilmore noted:

> Blacks have used Christianity not so much as it was delivered to them by racist white churches, but as its truth was authenticated to them in the experience of suffering and struggle, to reinforce an enculturated religious orientation and to produce an indigenous faith that emphasized dignity, freedom, and human welfare.[42]

The marriage between African religious traditions and American Christian Preaching was finally consummated nearly a century before the Second Great Awakening of the 1820-1830s, giving birth to a

---

[40] Henry H. Mitchell, *Black Belief: Folk Beliefs of Blacks in America and West Africa* (New York: Harper and Row, 1975), 15.

[41] Donald G. Mathews, *Religion in the Old South* (Chicago: University of Chicago Press, 1977), 226.

[42] Gayraud S. Wilmore, *Black Religion and Black Radicalism: An Interpretation of the Religious History of African Americans*, 3rd ed. rev. (New York: Orbis Books, 1999), 25.

mullotto child—the African American preacher who was distinguished by his Black preaching style. It was during the First Great Awakening (1730-1740s) that a religious synthesis took place in the life of the African slave in America through the preaching of some white revivalists like George Whitefield. The preaching of Whitefield predates the founding of the First African Baptist Church of Silver Bluff, South Carolina (1775), and the First Baptist Church of Williamsburg, Virginia (1776), which were two of the earliest established predominantly African American congregations. The autonomous governance and energetic preaching of the Black Church experience attracted both enslaved and freed African Americans who still identified with their ancestral roots of emotionalism and folk talk.[43]

The preaching style of George Whitefield stapled within the African American preacher an audacity to preach from within and not apart from his or her Africanness. In Whitefield, African American Christians and eventual preachers found shades of African oral traditions. Unlike his counterpart, Jonathan Edwards, and the majority of white preachers who were essayists, Whitefield was received and celebrated by blacks because of his tonality, sonorous voice, and dramatic and fervent style of preaching that included physical gesticulations. Whitefield was an Englishman whose extemporaneous preaching was partnered with his childhood interest in drama and free spiritedness that would manifest in him preaching in the open air. Whitefield's voice could put feelings into words.[44]

Vernon Loggins asserts, "The emotional preaching of Whitefield brought to the Negro a religion he could understand and which could

---

[43] Albert J. Raboteau, *Slave Religion: The Invisible Institution in the Antebellum South* (Oxford: Oxford University Press, 1978), 58.

[44] O.C. Edwards Jr., *A History of Preaching* (Nashville: Abingdon Press, 2004), 431-435.

stir him to self-expression."[45] This was the personification of communal identification as African Americans were now more willing to learn of this white man's religion. Whitefield was not primarily dramatic or emotional in his preaching style; to suggest that would be a disservice to his theological and homiletical aptitude. Whitefield's preaching was also appealing to the African American because it was relevant, deliberate, deductive, and essentially topical whereby he departed from a short text and used imaginative rhetorical techniques to communicate his own convictions with authority. This attraction to Whitefield's preaching by African Americans assisted in the shaping of the faith of African Americans as well as provided a few bricks for the building of Black Preaching.

Several African American preachers converted through the preaching of Whitefield and other white preachers, like Shubal Stearns and Daniel Marshall who preached throughout the Carolinas and Georgia. George Leille, who was influenced by their preaching, started the first African Baptist church of Silver Bluff, South Carolina, in 1773-1775 before organizing the first Black Baptist congregation in the Caribbean.[46] Leille's emotionally charged and rhetorically tonal preaching that fostered the first African Baptist Church of America also influenced black preachers like Andrew Bryan of Georgia, whom he baptized.[47]

The list of African American preachers who could tell the Christian story in their native rhetorical style dramatically increased between the

---

[45] Henry H. Mitchell, *Black Preaching: The Recovery of a Powerful Art* (Nashville: Abingdon Press, 1990), 32.

[46] Ibid., 33.

[47] Gayraud S. Wilmore, *Black Religion and Black Radicalism: An Interpretation of the Religious History of African Americans*, 3rd ed. rev. (New York: Orbis Books, 1999), 102.

periods of the First Great Awakening and the eventual 1866 signing of the Fourteenth Amendment, when the floodgates for African American constructed churches were opened. With the rise of independent Black churches, an inevitable right to practice their faith authentically followed. The secret meeting places in ravines and thickets by moonlight were converted to Black churches. A theology of both liberation and hope was joined together with a freedom of liturgical expression and an oral tradition of folk talk, to create a common tongue among African American worshippers. Eddie S. Glaude, Jr. stated the role independent Black worship played as a means for communal identification:

> The worship ceremonies within most of these institutions—the liturgies, the singing and dancing—invented, maintained, and renewed senses of communal identification that celebrated, even reveled in the uniqueness of black people and their relation to God.[48]

Glaude depicts the dynamics of the Antebellum Black religious experience during the days when the distinctiveness of African heritage was evident and celebrated in Christian worship services. The particularities of the Black worship experience (i.e., liturgies, singing, dancing) formed and further perpetuated a communal identification that was common throughout Black America. The liturgical expressions of the ancestral African American Christian were common among Baptists and Methodists. This further fuels the assertion that the contemporary autonomous and culture-pleasing Black Church has lost some of its "holy." The liturgical sayings and expressions of yesteryear have been in some cases totally reassembled into modern language that

---

[48] Eddie S. Glaude, Jr. "Of the Black Church and the Making of a Black Public," in *African American Religious Thought: An Anthology*, ed. Cornel West and Eddie S. Glaude Jr. (Louisville: Westminster John Knox Press, 2003), 347.

is somewhat disconnected from our ancestral roots. As a result, there is no longer a common tongue or sermonic song among Black churches that can cause both the young and old to dance in the Spirit. Present-day theories and tactics of persuasion have replaced Black Sacred Rhetoric and other ancestral liturgical expressions as the mode of communal identification.

This renaissance of folk theology and holy utterances of the past is not about time travel, nor is it anti-intellectual nostalgia. It is however an attempt to conserve a rapidly deteriorating oral tradition and belief system.[49] If folk theology was of great value during the Reconstruction as it encouraged, informed, comforted, and convicted a trans-generational and transitory community of African Americans, then its new form of Black Preaching can have substantive meaning today to those who recognize its theological and liturgical richness.

Kenneth Burke, a rhetorician and author of *The Rhetoric of Religion: Studies in Logology* stated, "Religion falls under the head of rhetoric in the sense that rhetoric is the art of persuasion."[50] Religious language is formed for communicative purposes. In this sense, religious exhortation is a constituent of rhetorical persuasiveness. In order to compel a specific community to respond to God or a human need, the preacher must be masterful in the folk language of the people. As Glaude noted, religious communal identification was determined according to the unique liturgies and verbal/non-verbal religious practices of Black people.[51] In this regard, persuasion is overrated or in fact does not exist.

---

[49] Nicholas Cooper-Lewter and Henry H. Mitchell, *Soul Theology: The Heart of American Black Culture* (Nashville: Abingdon Press, 1986), 157.

[50] Kenneth Burke, *The Rhetoric of Religion: Studies in Logology* (Berkeley: University of California Press, 1961), v.

[51] Cornel West, "American Africans in Conflict: Alienation in an Insecure Culture," in *African American Religious Thought: An Anthology*, ed. Cornel West and Eddie S. Glaude Jr. (Louisville: Westminster John Knox Press, 2003), 86.

Communal identification is the key that starts genuine dialogue. Communal identification precedes an individual's or group's willingness to follow a particular vision. Once the preacher identifies him or herself as one who knows the language or tradition of the people, particularly within the experienced Black Baptist Church, the preacher is better able to provoke a change or infuse the community with new ideas and concepts.

Communal association is the vehicle to change; unfortunately relationships between pastors and their people never materialized because of the language barriers arising from a postmodern approach to the eradication of "Grandma's Theology" in order to keep up with the times. Many distinctive traditions have been swept under the carpet of postmodernism, as nothing remains longstanding. There are many faults that can be found in the historicity of the religion of our fore-fathers and mothers; however, some of the theologically sound and colorful rhetoric as well as worship models that helped catechize the newly baptized and shape the faith of an African American people must remain holy. Folk theology in the form of Black Sacred Rhetoric should be reverenced and re-introduced to the church through liturgical preaching.

It was the grace of God in the form of church independence that "promoted the proliferation of African styles and manners within the Black Christian tradition and liturgy."[52] This gift of independently controlled churches would however be accompanied with an eventual threat in the maintenance, integrity, and care of these ancestral practices. First and positively, Cornel West suggested that the autonomous nature of the Black Baptist Church granted it the independence and sovereignty to change the organizational polity from

---

[52] Ibid.

a bureaucratic and hierarchical model to a congregational (tribal) and democratic structure to best accommodate and offer religious equality to the Black community. This religious freedom also made room for an African-influenced liturgy. This Africanized liturgical preaching may not had been publicly communicated by all African American preachers, particularly those who had white audiences watching both near and afar. Some African American preachers, then as today, chose to be more American than African. There is a double-consciousness, but one ought not to be ashamed of either part of the split-self. The African American preacher who preaches black has a message for the world.[53]

Harry "Black Harry" Hoosier preached to large crowds of Whites from 1784 to the turn of the ninetieth century whereby he preached a particular rhetorical style to whites as opposed to black audiences. Nevertheless, the white listeners would stay and hear this traveling revivalist.[54] John Jasper in the succeeding years was another African American preacher, as was Charles "The Black Spurgeon" Walker, who exercised publicly Africanness in preaching. Jasper was noted as one whose call to ministry was mediated through his master, but he still personified Black folk preaching of his day with intonation, call-and-response, hand gestures, shouting, and the ability to handle great words when he wanted to. He could also "talk in the old way," as he loved to do. Charles T. Walker, a learned man who matriculated through the former

---

[53] DuBois defines double-consciousness as this sense of always looking at one's self through the eyes of others or measuring one's soul by the tape of a world that looks on in amused contempt. He diagnosed the American Negro as having the feeling of "twoness" in that he does not want to Africanize America, for America has too much to teach the world and Africa. He also would not bleach his Negro soul, for he knows that Negro blood has a message for the world. He simply wants to be both a Negro and an American, as cited in W.E.B DuBois, *The Soul of Black Folk* (New York: Bantam Books, 1903), 3.

[54] Henry H. Mitchell, *Black Preaching: The Recovery of a Powerful Art* (Nashville: Abingdon Press, 1990), 25-26.

Atlanta Baptist Seminary, had the command of both white and black listeners but was unapologetically black and "Negro in every drop of his blood."[55] Walker used the language of the heart and ardent exhortation to proclaim the Gospel. These are a few that presented themselves as preachers of African descent. There were however countless nameless Black preachers that were not as comfortable or convicting in publicly preaching their Africanness and black style of preaching.

The stratification in the public preaching of African Americans as opposed to authentic Black Preaching was realized in the "hush harbor" era. Black believers would steal away after public worship services in White churches—that even had on occasion Black preachers—in order to fully express themselves religiously without the threat of being flogged. These clandestine wooded worship services kept alive African styles of worship. This Black church independence consequentially birthed an either/or liturgical dilemma—white or black liturgical practices. Unfortunately many chose and are still choosing mainstream appeal instead of ancestral values and practices. The preaching ministries of "Black Harry" Hoosier, John Jasper, and "The Black Spurgeon" Walker showcase the credibility of vernacular rhetoric and stylish oral transmission as a medium of communal identification; but as stated above some preachers who had tremendous visibility are not noted as possessing and presenting the same style of preaching.[56]

---

[55] From Robert Stuart McArthur's *Introduction to Life of Charles T. Walker, D.D. ("The Black Spurgeon") Pastor of Mt. Olivet Baptist Church, New York City* (1960), cited by O.C. Edwards in a chapter on *"The Fruits of Fervor"*—a synopsis of African American Christian Preaching fathers that include John Jasper, Charles T. Walker, Lemuel Haynes, and Charles Albert Tindley—in Edwards' *A History of Preaching* (Nashville: Abingdon Press, 2004), 532.

[56] This is an anecdotal assertion based upon my interpretation of the history of preaching and the personalities, styles, and responses of the aforementioned preachers. The primary sources of my interpretation are cited in *A History of Preaching, Black Preaching: The Recovery of a Power Art,* and an interview with Henry H. Mitchell.

Lemuel Haynes exemplified sound and liberating preaching but one who was not chronicled as black in style. Haynes was fathered by a black man and abandoned by his white mother. A white church deacon raised Lemuel from an early age. Haynes was educated and privileged to serve as pastor of white congregations. Haynes fought for freedom against slavery; his sermons, however, centered on Calvinistic doctrinal truths such as universal salvation.[57] Perhaps, to no fault of his own, there are no documented proofs of Haynes displaying an African influenced preaching style.

A certain lack of convergence implicit in the autonomy of the Black church experience, particularly within the Baptist denomination, makes it difficult to insure that the Africanness of our preaching will be executed. Shouting and holy laughter as well as folk preaching were common among both slaves and white revivalists. There is however no evidence that blacks, freed or enslaved, were openly expressive in the predominantly white church experience. More importantly, the religious rhetoric and preaching within white churches were homogenous and void of African influence with exception to some charismatic white revivalists. As a result, the invisible institution and "hidden churches" led by either literate or illiterate African-American preachers were erected so that blacks could freely and genuinely worship through gesture and rhetoric.

African Americans preferred their own meetings more than white church liturgy. The vivid imagery, dramatic delivery, use of repetition, parallelisms, gesture, rhythmic cadence, the holy whine, and a whole range of oratorical devices were used by whites such as Whitefield, but were second nature to Black Preaching. If Richard Allen's 1816 establishment of the African Methodist Episcopal church was the

---

[57] Ibid., 531.

inception of Black governed ecclesial authority, than "hush harbors" became the commencement, incubator, and seminary for the Africanization of Christian liturgical preaching.[58] From out of this freedom of religious expression and clandestine places of worship, the most illiterate and biblically unlearned neophytes formed a new religious vernacular that combined memorized biblical language with lived experience to form Negro spirituals and what I consider Black Sacred Rhetoric. It may not have been identical to what was in the Bible, but it was still God talk for a people who knew of God both pre and post Christian conversion.

Black Preaching by Definition

What is Black Preaching? Black Preaching or African American Preaching has a gamut of working definitions. Although synonymous with African American, Black more boldly suggests the tradition of folk theology as transmitted through oral traditions and celebratory cadences and gestures. Most definitions are in relation to style, theological significance, and anthropological relevance. In *What's the Matter with Preaching Today?* Cleophus J. Larue has catalogued a number of definitions of Black Preaching by both African American and White homileticians. Larue felt a need to identify Black Preaching as an ideal remedy for bad preaching. In Larue's account, according to William B. McClain, Black Preaching (1) has a sound biblical emphasis, and is (2) prophetic, (3) poetic in style, (4) dialogical, (5) declarative as opposed to suggestive, (6) life-situational, and (7) hopeful. Furthermore, Larue

---

[58] Richard Allen is the founder of the African Methodist Episcopal Church, which is the first predominantly Black denomination.

notes James Earl Massey who identifies five features of the Black sermon: the Black sermon is functional, festive, communal, radical, and climatic.[59]

Larue goes on to note others, like the pre-eminent father of Black homiletics, Henry H. Mitchell. Mitchell names three primary characteristics of Black Preaching: intonation in the form of whooping as an extremity of Black preaching, spontaneous responses to the movement of the Spirit accompanied with the expression of deep feelings, and finally the narrative invitation by which persons are invited to experience the sermon. Black Preaching is not an argument, but it is an art that invokes experience. Thomas Troeger and Evans Crawford cite call-and-response as distinctive to African American Preaching. Cleophus Larue in his own words defined the content of Black Preaching as a product of "a biblical hermeneutic of a sovereign God who acts powerfully on the part of the disinherited."[60]

Larue writes:

> This is not to suggest that the things that go on in this style are unique to black preaching or done by all black preachers, but it is to say that when taken together they come to the fore with such clarity and presence that one would not err in saying that these are some of the things you find repeatedly in the best of black preaching.[61]

As recorded by Katie Geneva Cannon, the late Isaac Rufus Clark described preaching as "divine activity wherein the Word of God is proclaimed or announced on contemporary issues for an ultimate

---

[59] Cleophus J. Larue, "Two Ships Passing in the Night," in *What's the Matter with Preaching Today?* ed. Mike Graves (Louisville: Westminster John Knox Press, 2004), 139-140.

[60] Ibid., 140.

[61] Ibid., 139.

41

response to our God." Cannon continues Clark's description of preaching (black preaching) as being a dialogue and "you ain't preaching if you are not answering the needs of the folk for whom you are raising these questions in their minds."[62] Black Preaching by definition is not a lecture or essay, but an experience and lively conversation between God, the preacher, and the pew that deals with real up-in-your-face issues. In the shadows of Cicero and later Augustine's view of orator and his or her purpose, I see the preacher as well as one who teaches, delights, and moves the listeners.[63]

Fueled and influenced by the voices, my working definition of preaching for the purpose of this thesis is that preaching in general is a sacramental act. Black Preaching is the naming of grace and disgrace through the vernacular rhetoric, images, and gestures of a particular people for the purpose of memorializing God's salvific work in the past, invoking God's liberating movement now, and moving a people toward the better.[64] The preacher serves as a mediator of meaning and translator of divine truths into folk talk. The preacher, no matter how upright his or her ēthos may be, does not invent the Word. The Word is birthed through the experience of God and a people/person. André

---

[62] Katie Geneva Cannon, *Teaching Preaching: Isaac Rufus Clark and Black Sacred Rhetoric* (New York: Continuum, 2002), 32, 41.

[63] Saint Augustine, *Saint Augustine On Christian Teaching*, trans. R.P.H. Green (Oxford: Oxford University Press, 1997), 117.

[64] Reader's Note: My reference to "naming grace" within the human experience is a derivative interpretation of Mary Catherine Hilkert's interpretation of sacramental imagination as the celebrating of the mystery of God's presence in the here and now, while summoning creation to a new future. Hilkert lists three qualifications of describing preaching as "naming grace": the experience to be named is a human experience; the reality that most persons' experience of God is in the face of, and in spite of, human suffering; and finally the interpretative keys to identifying are in the biblical story and symbols of Christian tradition. This is where I slightly differ in that I believe that a people's experience and folk theology can also be used to name grace. For a fuller discussion see: Mary Catherine Hilkert, *Naming Grace: Preaching and the Sacramental Imagination* (New York: Continuum, 1997), 46-49.

Resner says "God reveals, the preacher sees, and tells."[65] Intonation, imagination, and a celebratory style in its delivery is a given.

Substance or Style

The style and delivery of Black Preaching is embedded in many of the noted definitions. Just a Cleo Larue reminds us of the old adage: the soul of Black Preaching is emotional and *"starts slow, rises high, strikes fire, and sits down in a storm"*; style is about delivery.[66] Many old-school preachers are masters of this distinctive art. Gayraud S. Wilmore reported this striking distinctiveness:

> Every Sunday in the churches of the black community—North and South—old-style preachers exercise that same restraint, bringing their congregations to the height of religious hysteria with the "gravy" of homiletical peroration, and at the climax "sitting down in the storm." The traditional preacher knows when enough is enough....[67]

The homiletic, method, or style of Black Preaching from its conception has been tonal, manifestly imaginative, deeply emotive, vivid in imagery, dialogical, gesticulating, dialectical, and celebratory. The celebration should not be mistaken for "emotional expressiveness." Celebration is both style and substance in that it is parallel to delivery but has a theological significance: Black Preaching, and all preaching for

---

[65] André Resner Jr., *Preacher and Cross: Person and Message in Theology and Rhetoric* (Grand Rapids: William B. Eerdmans Publishing Company, 1999), 59.

[66] Cleophus J. Larue, *The Heart of Black Preaching* (Louisville: Westminster John Knox Press, 2000), 11.

[67] Gayraud S. Wilmore, *Black Religion and Black Radicalism: An Interpretation of the Religious History of African Americans*, 3rd ed. Revised (New York: Orbis Books, 1999), 74.

that matter, proclaims the Good News to a sinfully captive world. The tone is to therefore be joyful and celebratory while communicating the Good News. Preaching which has kerygmatic fulfillment in proclaiming that Jesus conquered death and *got up eeeaaarly one Sunday morning,* deserves to be pronounced with glee and elation. It is in our belief in Jesus' resurrection that we find hope in being raised from our proverbial graves. Celebratory preaching is jubilant and void of a contrite monotone voice as to be ashamed of the Gospel or one with no hope. I concur with Mitchell in that celebration expresses gladness about what God has done. The "has done" is the affirmation taught throughout the main body of the sermon; whether it's God's saving grace, healing grace, or forgiving grace.[68] Preaching is a holy undertaking and humbling experience. The revelation of God through the finite person of the preacher causes the preacher's testimony to be one of celebration as he or she comes to a close and looks back and wonders, *"How I made it over...it was nobody but the Lord."*

Martin King was a master of delivery. King's preaching was inarguably of theological substance, but he also mastered the style of Black Preaching and the standard features of sound which included: alliteration, metaphor, assonance, anaphora, epistrophe, syncopated stammering, crescendo, and intonation.

1. *Alliteration* is the repetition of the first sound of several words in a line.
2. *Metaphor* signifies language that juxtaposes entities that initially provoke puzzlement.
3. *Assonance* is the repetition of similar vowel sounds followed by different consonants.[69]

---

[68] Henry H. Mitchell, *Celebration and Experience in Preaching* (Nashville: Abingdon Press, 1990), 63-66.

[69] Richard Lischer, *The Preacher King: Martin Luther King Jr. and the Word that*

4. *Anaphora* begins successive clauses with the same group of words.
5. *Epistrophe* ends successive clauses with the same group of words.
6. *Syncopated stammering* is the deliberate stuttered pauses between groups of words.[70]
7. *Crescendo* is a gradual increase in sound.
8. *Intonation* is the variation of pitch that provides melody in speech.

The preaching of Black Sacred Rhetoric is not necessarily about style but more so is about substantive judgments about God's grace or our hope in God that is inscribed within these holy sayings. Black Sacred Rhetoric is not a dialect as is Black English or Ebonics, with spellings being altered to read as they sound and meanings being coded as they evolve with popular culture. Black Sacred Rhetoric is God-talk that requires exegesis and the mediation of Black Preaching. It can however be spoken apart from liturgy.

The style of Black Preaching enhances the depth of Black Sacred Rhetoric's meaning and value, but these utterances are fully capable of standing on their own with or without cadenced and sonorous voice inflection and precise and appropriate hand gestures. Like Negro Spirituals, minus the singing, Black Sacred Rhetoric is an interpretative response to a particular human situation. Both spirituals and Black Sacred Rhetoric, although not directly peeled from the pages of the Bible are in fact like canon to the Black Christian experience. Black Sacred Rhetoric expresses not only trouble, but also a hope, enduring faith, a call for a human response, and deliverance by God (i.e., *trouble don't last always; you do your part and God will do the rest*).[71] This is the substance of the preaching of Black Sacred Rhetoric.

Moved America (Oxford: Oxford University Press, 1995), 122-128.

[70] O.C. Edwards Jr., *A History of Preaching* (Nashville: Abingdon Press, 2004), 709-710.

[71] Brian K. Blount, *Cultural Interpretation: Reorienting New Testament Criticism* (Minneapolis: Fortress Press, 1995), 55.

Black Sacred Rhetoric

Theologically sound, biblically accurate, and congregationally colorful and relevant preaching is not as obsolete as some have suggested. If you were to pin your ear to the winds of a Sunday morning, you would hear such preaching being echoed from many clandestine-typed pulpits that are invisible in the sight of mainstream and popular preaching. There are countless voices—unsung "heroes" and "sheroes" whose preaching is indeed the last expression of theology and whose theology is made proclamatory through both philosophical and folk traditions.

Negro Spirituals as Preamble to Black Sacred Rhetoric

Negro Spirituals were in most cases expressions of religious faith as well as socio-political protest and banter. Slaves who were forbidden to speak and worship in their native tongue countered their oppression by creating impromptu musicality in the genre of spirituals.

Howard Thurman suggested that the Negro Spiritual was a reflection of a people's interpretation of love, life, and death. The understanding of the slaves' religious experience was the clue to unraveling the meaning of many of the spirituals.[72] There was a theological and anthropological conviction being articulated in each spiritual. The dialect of these spirituals was, however, varied. According to James Weldon Johnson, "The idioms and pronunciation of the dialect varied in different sections of the South."[73] This is so with Black Sacred

---

[72] Howard Thurman, "The Negro Spiritual Speaks of Life and Death: Love," in *African American Religious Thought: An Anthology*, ed. Cornel West and Eddie S. Glaude, Jr. (Louisville: Westminster John Knox Press, 2003), 29.

[73] James Weldon Johnson and J. Rosamund Johnson, *The Book of American Negro Spirituals* (New York: The Viking Press, 1925), 43.

Rhetoric, as well. Black Sacred Rhetoric from a Pentecostal church in the Bayou may be different from the Black Church idiom of a Baptist church in rural North Carolina or downtown Chicago. The testimonial voices of the spirituals echoed how a people of suffering were able to speak of majesty, beauty, and power. Negro Spirituals are the cradle of liberation theology and of Black Sacred Rhetoric. Songs like "Swing Low, Sweet Chariot," "I Want to Be Ready," and "Steal Away to Jesus," signaled that the time for escape was at hand. "Wade in the Water" by Marlena Shaw gave travel instructions for avoiding capture as the Ohio River and Mississippi became the Jordan River.

> *Now if you should get there before I do*
> *(I know) God's gonna trouble the water*
> *Tell all my friends that I'm comin' too*
> *(I know) God's gonna trouble the water.*[74]

The Negro Spiritual was also a vernacular of faith and a coded concession of how African Americans believed that this unseen, but just, God was going to deliver them from the sins of slavery. These spirituals were arranged by both slaves and post-emancipation African Americans as "an interpretive response to their particular human circumstance."[75] The lyrics were Christianized in that they possessed biblical imagery. Brian K. Blount noted:

> They begin with the horrors of their experience and then interpret those horrors through their understanding of biblical images.... The Bible becomes an interpretative means rather than an interpretative end.... Biblical images therefore required further and "corrected" ideational interpretation if they were to be used in a serviceable way

---

[74] Ibid.
[75] Ibid.

> by slaves.... Biblical language, in the form of conceptual ideas, was not simply used because it was biblical—and therefore somehow sacred—but because it helped to bring meaning and understanding to their sociohistorical circumstance.[76]

This imaginative interpretation of the biblical texts also presented itself into folk talk and Black Sacred Rhetoric. The Negro spiritual continued to develop late into the mid-twentieth century. The Civil Rights Movement of the 1960s brought "We Shall Overcome" and "This Little Light of Mine" into the liturgical speech of countless Black churches. A myriad of interpretations of the biblical text were introduced to the religious experience of African Americans as holy sayings. The Negro Spiritual and Black Sacred Rhetoric are like *"topoi"* and the places where African Americans' religious traditions, wisdom, and truths are stored.[77] Topoi are those widely accepted and normative axioms within a community.

What is wrong with Black Preaching?

A disconnect from the holy is a devil's workshop in Black Preaching. Preaching that lacks distinctiveness, imaginative appeal, and a striking force is bad preaching. It is not Black Preaching. Black Preaching is guilty of sometimes lacking cross-generational relevancy or failing to make practical interpretations of divine truths for all hearers.

The listening ear must be awakened and re-trained through consistent and sound illustrative old-school preaching that is in new

---

[76] Brian K. Blount, *Cultural Interpretation: Reorienting New Testament Criticism* (Minneapolis: Fortress Press, 1995), 56-57.

[77] Richard Lischer, *The Preacher King: Martin Luther King Jr. and The Word that Moved America* (New York: Oxford University Press, 1995), 94.

form. Fred Craddock believes that television has changed the human sensorium: "The visual has removed the oral from the field, or at least has created a crisis between the eye and ear."[78] Poor hearing is in fact a result of placing more value in what one sees. Many socially elite white-church-in-blackface liturgical settings are now being looked upon as normative, whether sound preaching is coming from the ambo or not. The preacher can assist in the re-training of the ear by vividly communicating "Grandma's Theology" to a visually focused world. The ear will better appreciate folk theology and Black Sacred Rhetoric if the oral to aural transmission is colorful and relevant.

E. Franklin Frazier credited assimilation as the culprit of an early twentieth century exodus of socio-economically advancing blacks from their ancestral culture. As assimilated African Americans rose to middle-class status, they in return rejected the folk heritage and sought to slough off any reminders of their folk inheritance and heritage.[79] Perhaps this is why Black Sacred Rhetoric is vanishing from African American liturgical settings.

Frazier further noted how the Colored Methodist Episcopal Church changed its name to Christian Methodist Episcopal Church, foregoing its ancestral lineage. The good news is that this was not the case among all African Americans. A notable stance in the form of a revolt was taken when there were talks of changing African to American in the naming of the African Methodist Episcopal Church. A position is now being taken to keep the Africanness in Black Christian preaching in the form of Black Sacred Rhetoric. There is a community that has an appetite for it and is

---

[78] Fred B. Craddock, *As One Without Authority*, Revised and with New Sermons (St. Louis: Chalice Press, 2001), 9.

[79] E. Franklin Frazier, "The Negro Church and Assimilation," in *African American Religious Thought: An Anthology*, ed. Cornel West and Eddie S. Glaude, Jr. (Louisville: Westminster John Knox Press, 2003), 70.

simply not having church without it.[80]

The oral traditions and sayings of African Americans, both sacred and secular, serve as a fundamental vehicle for "getting over" according to Geneva Smitherman. Smitherman furthered her argument for African American linguistics by suggesting that oral traditions preserve the African American heritage and "reflects the collective spirit of the race through song, story, folk sayings and rich verbal interplay among everyday people." Furthermore, life and survival lessons that inevitably raise hope are handed down from generation to generation to a particular people through a particular vernacular.[81] Although Black Sacred Rhetoric transcends the institutional church and liturgical preaching as it is spoken in the kitchen, corn fields, jails, and street corners, the mediation of its contemporary meaning should be exercised by the preacher. This is paramount in order to help reshape the aural aptitude of the listeners of this vernacular rhetoric.

In *Soul Theology*, Nicolas Cooper-Lewter and Henry Mitchell tell the story of a 1972 arrested drug lord named Luke who was incarcerated in a New Orleans jail cell along with numerous conspirators and partners in crime. All eyes fell on Luke who unlike others was allowed to keep his belt and watch. With eyes cast upon him he spoke out and said: "They remove your belt to keep you from hanging yourself.... They could give me a rope, and I wouldn't hang myself for *God has never put a thing on this earth that he didn't make man strong enough to withstand.*" Cooper-Lewter and Mitchell also referenced a 1979 Jet magazine interview with Lola Falana who was asked how she was able to manage such a demanding Las Vegas schedule. She responded in Black Sacred Rhetoric,

---

[80] Ibid.

[81] Geneva Smitherman, *Talkin and Testifyin: The Language of Black America* (Detroit: Wayne State University Press, 1977), 73.

"He (God) gives you no more than you can carry." The interpretation of this non-biblical God-talk that was uttered from the pulpit of a New Orleans jail cell and Las Vegas club was a trust in the providence of God. Cooper-Lewter and Mitchell cite:

> God is provident in the limits set or built into life.... Luke the dope dealer expressed belief in a parallel limit when he declared that God would not let more come upon him than he could deal with. He was, likely, paraphrasing a gospel song, "He Knows Just How Much You can Bear," based on 1 Cor. 10:13, written in the depression by Roberta Martin.[82]

A revival of folk heritage and "blackenized" vernacular religious rhetoric that is made relevant and plain is needed in order to help rebound and distinguish Black Preaching as a dispenser of not only the Gospel of Jesus Christ, but also God-embedded folk talk. More African American preachers need to practice Black Preaching. In light of dwindling Sunday school attendance and youngsters no longer freely sitting at the feet of their elders, a lot of Africanized idioms, proverbs, customs, and attitudes are not being passed on.[83] For the many African Americans who have not been assimilated into other liturgical settings and who like to hear the preacher "talk that talk," Black Sacred Rhetoric helps shape their reality.

---

[82] Nicholas Cooper-Lewter and Henry H. Mitchell, *Soul Theology: The Heart of American Black Culture* (Nashville: Abingdon Press, 1986). 1-2, 19.

[83] Geneva Smitherman, *Talkin and Testifyin: The Language of Black America* (Detroit: Wayne State University Press, 1977), 90.

Chapter 3

Excavating the Truth

Establishing truth oftentimes takes more than one person's viewpoint. Various truths have always existed but required collective voices and sometimes persons of greater influence to concur on their reality and distinctiveness. Every genre of music, style of writing, and expression of art may have been initiated by one revolutionist who dared to be different and create what he or she imaginatively composed or witnessed in others. Someone has to be the first to formally name certain created realities as well as properly introduce them to a larger audience.

The Negro Spiritual is a perfect example. The singing of Negro Spirituals long preceded their public affirmation. Negro Spirituals were first sung by African American slaves as religious expression and coded rebellion against slavery. Spirituals were hummed and sung throughout the southern and northern slave fields of the early nineteenth century by countless slaves of undying faith. These spirituals were not formally recognized as a genre of music until a white minister heard this phenomenal music being sung by two of his slaves. These spirituals went on to be performed by the Jubilee Singers of Fisk University in 1871 and later published in a book one year later.[84]

---

[84] During the 1850s while serving as superintendent at the Spencer Academy of Choctaw Nation, the Reverend Alexandria Reid heard two slaves singing "Swing Low, Sweet Chariot," "Steal Away to Jesus," and "I'm a Rolling" to name a few. After attending a concert and hearing the melodious voices of several Negro students from Fisk

Black Sacred Rhetoric

Identifying certain longstanding non-biblical holy sayings that are consistently used in Black Preaching and in other non-liturgical settings demand the same attention as once given to Negro Spirituals in order to formally staple them into the historical fabric of Black Preaching. A collective attempt to assemble these holy sayings and authenticate their consistent and meaningful usage must be established. These holy sayings as Black Sacred Rhetoric and as canon unto the Black Church require historical appropriation and affirmation from homiletical experts of our faith. Likewise, observations and accounts from laity are essential to validate such a claim.

Various approaches have been taken in order to establish Black Sacred Rhetoric as a legitimate and nationally recognized happening within the Black Church experience. The primary point of my departure has been based on my own cultural encounters of hearing and using Black Sacred Rhetoric as a means to illustrate or expound upon the propositional truths of biblical and topical sermons. This has been a personal, face-to-face journey extending over seven years. The focus became more formal and intentional, however, over the past two years.

I can easily recall initially hearing these holy utterances in church service and from the lips of my mother and grandmother, dating back over a quarter of a century. This book and its ultimate purposes have also heightened my awareness of such a Black Church canon. I cannot escape from hearing Black Sacred Rhetoric while at church, tuning in a gospel station, or merely talking to my elders. I am pleased to hear it when it is appropriately interjected, and in the same manner it pains me

---

University. Reid later transcribed the Negro Spirituals that he heard his two slaves sing ("Uncle" Wallace Willis and "Aunt" Minerva Willis as they were referred to) and gave them to these Jubilee Singers of Fisk University who later performed them in 1871. Many of these songs were then published in 1872 by Thomas F. Steward in the book *Jubilee Songs as Sung by the Jubilee Singers of Fisk University.*

when it is exploited or left to stand on its own. As preacher and hearer of preaching, I recounted the times when I used the saying *"He's my bridge over troubled waters"* while preaching from biblical texts whereby waterways were presented as barriers during transitions in life. My recollections led me to notice how the congregational response increased in "amens, yes sirs, say its, and preach preachers." While observing masters of Black Sacred Rhetoric like the revivalist in Chapter 1, I was amazed to see how *"ain't He alright!"* echoed louder and invoked praise both from the young and old alike—perhaps even more so than "For God so loved the world that He gave His only begotten Son, and whosoever believes in Him shall not perish but will have everlasting life" (John 3:16). These experiences carried me into deeper discovery of this event in Black Preaching.

The ethnographic appraisal spans through Central and Northeastern rural Virginia, to Baltimore, with additional eye-witness accounts from parts of North Carolina and St. Louis, Missouri to our Nation's capital. Based on my cultural observations, I framed and asked the question, "If occasionally used, can this vernacular rhetoric aid in the building of trusted relationship between preacher (me) and the pew (older member)?" As mentioned in Chapter 1, I have been privileged to spend a lot of time preaching in my beloved and childhood rural church setting. On many occasions while preaching at revivals or other special services, I distinctively noticed within the eyes of some members an initial disconnect between us. My face is young, and I suppose they expected only contemporary words to flow from it. Unintentionally at first, I just naturally used Black Sacred Rhetoric in my introductory sermon statements and, in some instances, a few in my celebratory closure. The chilling waters of the perceived generational chasm were heated, and I was looked upon as one of them in most cases. My personality now commanded respect as a true man of God. I associated this with not only my ēthos, or relative strength of character in preaching, but also with the appropriation of Black Sacred Rhetoric as a means of communal identification.

Further research was required in the form of collective voices of the Black Church experience. Truth oftentimes requires a second opinion. My experiences were not unique; therefore I wanted to validate them through a host of voices. In addition, I wanted to name a suitable number of these holy sayings that we all would agree upon as having their place in Black Preaching. I decided to target fifty-five of these colloquial idioms in order to align one with each Sunday of the Black Church calendar year as well as one for each service of Watch Night, Ash Wednesday, and Good Friday. This lectionary of sayings will concretize Black Sacred Rhetoric and hopefully establish it as supportive text for Black Preaching. Although this might be blasphemous to some, Isaac Rufus Clark demonstratively suggested, "Every text does not have to come from the Bible."[85] In addition, Clark believed that Christian hymns, for example, could serve as preaching texts after critical theological judgment has been made. To follow the philosophy of Clark, Black Sacred Rhetoric may very well be justified in standing as a singular text for Black Preaching. I am however set on partnering this para-canon of culturally accepted truths with biblical texts that share a similar theological perspective. The praxis of Soul Theology is demonstrated in several of these forthcoming testimonials that chronicle the usage of what Henry Mitchell classifies as "Aunt Jane's Theology" in order to connect with a speculative community of faith.

---

[85] Katie Geneva Cannon, *Teaching Preaching: Isaac Rufus Clark and Black Sacred Rhetoric* (New York: Continuum, 2002), 69-70.

Authenticating the Word

This commentary has been supported by the invaluable insights and authentic experiences of several persons who teamed in my effort to give Black Sacred Rhetoric its proper forum. Many voices have attested to the praxis of this folk tradition including pastors whose religious origin is of Louisiana, California, Alabama, South Carolina, North Carolina, Georgia, and Maryland. A discover of this Trans-Atlantic rhetoric was made in my travels throughout Ghana. From Kumasi to Cape Coast and in Accra in particular, Christian preachers were heard proclaiming "The Lord will make a way somehow" and "You don't miss your water until your well runs dry" as well as distinctive colloquial sayings that were pronounced in preaching such as "An empty bag cannot stand upright." After years of group thinking, collective reflection, and continuous attentiveness to these proposed holy sayings, level ground has been found and a common language has been determined as theologically sound with the context of church although apart from scripture or doctrine.

Countless other sayings from other communities of faith are also constituents of Black folk theology. It is my hope that others will pick up their shovels and continue the dig before other valued holy sayings are left to die in the graves of postmodernism and the tombs of "deblackenized" preaching. The recovery of Black Preaching includes the preservation and preaching of Black Sacred Rhetoric. The words of wisdom that were shared via interviews and focus groups pertaining to religious rhetoric and the current and future states of Black Preaching have been interwoven throughout the preceding chapters. This chapter however presents and provides an interpretation of the measurable data collected from two surveyed communities of faith.

57

Findings

Ninety questionnaires were collected at the first site. The demographics were varied, as individuals were asked to identify their ministerial position, how often they preach their use of lectionaries for weekly sermonic preparations, their geographical location and denominational affiliation, and gender. The vast majority of the surveyed were Baptist (80 percent) pastors (57 percent) who preach weekly without an allegiance to lectionary readings. The Southern (55 percent) and Northeastern (24 percent) regions encompassed the majority of the surveyed ministers. Although 33 percent of the examined did not identify their gender on the questionnaires, those who did respond identified 44 percent male and 22 percent female, respectably.

The fifty-five non-biblical holy sayings identified by the focus group were listed with a response as to their usage: often, rarely, or never. The question was suited for those who had actually applied or heard these sayings in liturgical preaching. Each listed idiom had resounding responses from persons of all regions, denominational affiliations, gender, and ministerial position. Most obviously, pastors responded more frequently as those who employ these sayings as opposed to associate ministers who preach on occasion. Pastoral preaching more fittingly utilizes this Black Sacred Rhetoric for illustration or a means of communal identification. The pastor-preacher's repertoire of Black Sacred Rhetoric appears to be more comprehensive and active.

The second site gathered twenty-eight questionnaires for which all participants were Baptists from the Southern state of Virginia. Sixty percent qualified themselves as pastors who preach weekly. Eleven of these holy sayings were distinctive in that all surveyed clergypersons acknowledged their usage. The reverent laughter that noticeably filled the room while participating in the survey was evidence of a truth that had finally been revealed.

Interpretation

Based on the input from the two separate groupings of clergy and laypersons as well as the opinions that I have heard from laity and kinfolk, it is clear that these holy sayings have a place within the Black Church. Throughout the surveying process other non-biblical holy sayings have been divulged by the surveyed, such as, *"When I think of Jesus and all that He's done for me, once saved always saved," "This too shall pass,"* and, the rapidly spreading and popular *"Turn to your neighbor"* that promotes community, attentiveness, and witnessing. This further substantiates my claim that the work has been initiated but that further investigation is called for in order to name the totality of Black Sacred Rhetoric. It is my summation that although these fifty-five non-biblical declaratives solidify themselves as a para-canon, there are a few other books to be added. Many of these utterances are regional, in that some Midwesterners have shared with me that it wasn't until they traveled down south that they heard *"Ain't He alright"* melodiously declared from the Black pulpit, as well as several other holy sayings.

The aspect of gender has no bearing on the usage of this vernacular, nor does the gender exclusive language within some of these sayings. Black Sacred Rhetoric is a part of a folklore that goes beneath the surface of gender, denominationalism, and constituency. Black Sacred Rhetoric is a theology that is as much a part of the Black Church as are wedding nuptials and baptismal litanies. The face of folk theology is the face of the people who have experienced God and dare to articulate God's grandeur and their hope in God, in their own words.

Black Sacred Rhetoric has a home within the Black Church. The widespread recognition of these sayings, although predominantly southern, is still a microcosm of the entire Black Church. A sub-cultural oral tradition of God-talk exists and must be preserved as many Negro spirituals were, so that their invisible pages do not fade away. It should be reiterated however, that the usage and a congregations longing to hear from the para-canon or Grandma's Theology is shared both the so-called silk-stocking and mainstream churches as well as the clandestine and folk tradition churches. These religious vernacular or similar non-biblical sayings are also shared in the predominantly White Church experience as well. This has been echoed by some of my Caucasian brothers and sisters in Christ, in particular of the Baptist tradition.

Chapter 4

Going Backward in Order to Move Forward

This lectionary or devotional with brief commentary is a one-year calendric cycle of Black Sacred Rhetoric. Each holy saying is designated as the assigned reading for each of the fifty-two Sundays of the Black Church Year as listed in the *African American Heritage Hymnal*.[86] However, within this composition, the concluding Sunday of the fifty-two Sunday celebration is identified as Culmination Celebration as opposed to Watch Night Service. Homecoming Service has also been added to this Black Church Year as a Sunday of liturgical celebration. Homecoming Worship services are unique in Southern states as former members who relocated to Northern cities return home for community worship and ecclesial support in the bringing of special offerings. In addition to the fifty- two Sundays of the Black Church liturgical experience, three other worship celebrations are included. They are Ash Wednesday, Good Friday (Holy Week), and the aforementioned Watch Night Service, because of its various days of occurrence.

This particular lectionary of Black Sacred Rhetoric will start with the New Year and First Sunday Worship Celebration of Emancipation as opposed to the season of Advent. The Sundays within this lectionary are

---

[86] In addition to this compilation of Protestant hymnody that is presented in the African American religious tradition, litanies are also presented as liturgical readings for the "52 Sundays of Worshipful Celebration" in the Black Church Year as cited in Delores Carpenter and Nolan E. Williams, eds., *African American Heritage Hymnal* (Chicago: GIA Publications, 2001).

generally celebrated within the Black Church Year but not necessarily in the listed sequence. This calendric presentation is purposeful primarily for structure and for providing an ideal time to consider the meaning of this Black Church canon. Preaching according to this schedule is strictly voluntary, nevertheless a commentary for each sacred saying is aligned with a particular Worship Celebration as a challenge to thoughtfully interpret and inform the congregation of this valued religious vernacular. This lectionary is an attempt to formally present and concretize Black Sacred Rhetoric as a stable constituent of Black Worship. This work is my effort to "preserve in permanent form this treasure of faith" as it was Wyatt Tee Walker's successful intent to do the same for the *Prayer and Praise Hymns* of the Black religious experience.[87] This list of readings also represents and reinforces the already celebrated Black Church Calendar Year as a time and constant reminder of how God reveals Godself to the Black Church.[88]

The Black Sacred Rhetoric commentary offers meaningful interpretation of each one of the fifty-five holy sayings presented in the lectionary. The commentary is based on lived experience and the overhearing of the many voices and testimonies of those who have uttered these sacred unscripted words. Acknowledgement is given to those that were derived from our rich hymnological history. This commentary, however, offers in many cases both a holy perspective and an anthropological appeal to these often said but yet misinterpreted utterances.

The Word, in the sense of theological significance of this Black Sacred Rhetoric, is made plain in this composition. In order to combat

---

[87] Wyatt Tee Walker, *Spirits That Dwell in Deep Woods: The Prayer and Praise Hymns of the Black Religious Experience* (Chicago: GIA Publication, 1987), xx.

[88] The usage of *Godself* is to the capture and reference the totality and essence of God apart from gender exclusive language.

the misuse and cheapening of this God-talk, the listed meanings should be considered before using this Black Church canon. Just as hermeneutical tools are to be appropriately used to effectively and accurately exegete the world behind and of the biblical text, a contemplative attempt must be made to contextualize and communicate the valued truth of Black Sacred Rhetoric. In the words of James H. Harris: "The preacher must make it plain" in reference to the preaching of the Gospel as the Word of God.[89] In the case of the Black Church and its vernacular rhetoric, the Word is also Black Sacred Rhetoric.

---

[89] James H. Harris, *The Word Made Plain: the Power and Promise of Preaching* (Minneapolis: Fortress Press, 2004), ix.

Lectionary

A Commentary on Black Sacred Rhetoric
1st SUNDAY
Emancipation Day

He woke me up early this morning,
clothed in my right mind with blood
still running warm in my veins.[90]

To be awakened is to be aroused, alerted, or enlightened to the reality of one's valued existence and purpose in being. This moment of consciencenization shatters the silence of darkness and sinfulness as the new beginning and the God who is new every morning serves as evidence that the believer has made it through another period of utter obscurity. With a sound mind that is girded in both rationality and imagination, the believer now enters a new day fully alive in body, mind, and soul as he or she actively praises God through service and meaningful living. To be alive commands one to serve God through righteous and communal living. This statement is an announcement that God is the keeper of our lives and that the new mercies of each morning is oriented in God's grace. Daily, God calls humankind into being without the interruption of the looming night of death. The sound mindedness that is cloaked in reason and prudence recognizes its source as God. The blood that circulates throughout the vascular system carrying oxygen throughout the body is also critical in the expulsion of waste through the excretory channels. For this, the believer rejoices, as life is both sustained and cleansed.

---

[90] Nolan Williams. "The Lord is Blessing me Right Now," in *African American Heritage Hymnal*, ed. Delores Carpenter and Nolan E. Williams Jr. (Chicago: GIA Publications, 2001), 506.

2ⁿᵈ SUNDAY
Rev. Dr. Martin Luther King, Jr.

You can't make me doubt Him
because I know too much about Him.[91]

When one's conviction and hope in God has been tested and proved unwaveringly, there is very little room for doubt when new challenges are thrust upon him or her. For a believer to profess knowledge of God's salvific will as well as to know God for him or herself is evidence that the believer has experienced God's comforting love and delivering power. The bearing of Christ's cross encompasses persecution, public ridicule, and moments of isolation that could cause one to pause before going into even deeper waters, but for the believer, he or she is not halted by doubt. Disbelief does not resonate within the devotee's mind because he or she is convinced through the knowledge of God's Word that cross bearing is for Christ's sake. To be in the know, is to be certain in one's faith that God has promised success and vindication and deliverance to those who endeavor to serve God. The believer is not derailed by the threat of painful consequences or statistical proofs that would suggest an unlikelihood of positive outcomes.

To be in the knowledge of God is not made evident in the regurgitation of doctrinal truths or scripture but rather a faith that has been shaped by the former movements of God in the life of the witness. This belief in the mightiness of God is fixed in the mind of the believer as the believer chooses to rest in the unseen and take action without hesitation as opposed to settling with uncertainty and a lack of confidence when facing visible threats with a low probability of deliverance.

---

[91] Wyatt Tee Walker in his theological exposition of this hymnal frame noted that it possesses universal recognition in the historic Black Church. See Wyatt Tee Walker's *Spirits That Dwell in Deep Woods*, 202-205

3rd SUNDAY
Installation of Church Leaders

If you do right by people,
people will do right by you.

God created humanity in God's image with a purpose of being with, among, and for one another. A God-oriented love requires one to love one's neighbor as him or herself. This *pathos* or heartfelt conviction that feels the hurts and joys of the other creates an appetite within the believer to render kindness unto others because it in return strengthens one's own heart. Love must be placed into action. Love, much like respect, is a psychological constant that involves interaction and action. Words and saying "I love you" can affirm the beloved's need to feel cared for, but words oftentimes fall short of meeting the needs of our neighbors. The question must be raised: If I were in this predicament what would I like for others to do for me? This is in most cases the response that God expects the church to exhibit. Church Leadership specifically, serves as a mirror to the faith community it services. Treatment of others in a just, loving, and respectful manner will create an atmosphere of equality and attitude of admiration toward one another; however, a leadership that oppresses and religiously victimizes any segment of a faith community in return is asking its membership to do the same to it.

4th SUNDAY

Epiphany

He may not come when you want Him to,
but He's always right on time.

To the believer, waiting leads to a greater witness. The anticipatory movement of God is a pre-celebratory stage of perfecting one's faith. God is coming. The eschatological hope has been fastened to the believer's mind, but the wait births a dialectical dilemma. One's strong desires and wishes can lead to an untimely or premature expectation. A believer realizes that God's continuum of revelation and will to fulfill is in most cases unlike humanity's concept of timing. Anticipation, expectation, waiting, and eagerness are human enterprises that are predicated upon one's understanding and impatience with time. Humanity's perspective to time is most often *chronos* or chronological increments of duration whereby persons expect events to occur. God is however perfect timing (*kairos*) and reveals Godself at the right moment according to cosmic will and true human need. To place durational restraints on God is to suggest that God is inferior to created reality or existence, as opposed to suggesting in the words of Thomas Aquinas— *Deus non est existens, sed supra existentiam*: "God does not exist, God transcends all existence."[92] Waiting on God and believing that God will show up right on time instead of when an impatient humanity wants God to show up distinguishes believers from others and shows that time and circumstances are somehow both obsolete and revelatory to a God who is the very act of existence itself.

---

[92] Edward Schillebeeckx references Aquinas' *Summa Theologiae* in interpreting silence as the voice of God, as cited in Mary Catherine Hilkert and Robert J. Schreiter, *The Praxis of the Reign of God: An Introduction to the Theology of Edward Schillebeeckx*, with a prologue by Edward Schillebeeckx (New York: Fordham University Press, 2002), xiv.

5th SUNDAY

Black History Observance

Trouble don't last always.

Trouble is a disturbance or event that causes emotional or physical distress or pain. Many problems are manifested in the form of temporary unemployment due to layoffs or outsourcing, physiological changes that are diagnosed as diseases, as well as relational maladjustments in marriages or home life. Just as these quandaries have an origin, the believer rests upon the possibility that difficult days also have an end. Neither moments of ecstasy nor trouble are eternal. This is no pie in the sky unrealized eschatology but rather a distant reality of liberation. The dream of Martin Luther King, Jr. and its relative realization is evidence that even his proclaimed "difficult days" that would be ahead did not last always. The nation still hurts from the loss of King's life, but it has healed. Always is forever and only equates to God. The believer refuses to classify struggle as an eternal truth. The God of our people is absolutely eternal, pure positivity, and a constant source of future possibility.[93] Even if a particular strife-ridden predicament should lead to death, the trouble dies as well, but the faithful who have been promised eternity is carried to a realm that is free from distress and pain.

---

[93] Ibid., xxvi .

LENTEN SEASON
Ash Wednesday

I was sinking deep in sin, far from peaceful shore,
deeply stained within; sinking to rise no more,
but the Master of the sea heard my despairing cry.[94]

To sink is to drop beneath the surface of safety and to be removed from familiar settings and family. Sin creates an atmosphere of raging isolation and downward spiraling whereby death seems imminent and inevitable. This estrangement from God and violation of moral rule lends itself to a state of guilt-ridden introspective loneliness (I was sinking) where one feels all alone even in the company of loving supporters. The believer, however, is able to stand once again on the peaceful shores of self assurance and communal acceptance by calling upon and repenting back unto the God of deliverance. The omnipresence of God is in all places at all times and one's faithfulness in such an ever present and merciful God destroys the fear of drowning in one's past transgressions.

God responds to the prayers of those who stand in desperate need of rescue. Upon the seas or places of heightened danger, God hears the fervent prayers and silent tears of a sinking soul. The peaceful shore is where one longs to be. Although stability appears to be at a great distance, the God of creative love can bring about peace to one's drowning heart. God is Master of all created reality; both land and sea and good and bad.

---

[94] James Rowe. "Love Lifted Me," *African American Heritage Hymnal*, ed. Delores Carpenter and Nolan E. Williams Jr. (Chicago: GIA Publications, 2001), 504.

6th SUNDAY
Church Anniversary

We have come this far by faith. [95]

There will be times when believers (we) are unable to find solace in public domains or personal wealth. Although intellect, heritage, resourcefulness, and a God-fearing political constituency can be beneficial to a church's development, the Black Church specifically has been sustained by the grace of God as God uses the Black Church as an instrument of liberation and hope for others. When it is apparent that the church has been kept by a source much greater than itself, it galvanizes the believers into a collective profession of faith. The journey that most Black churches have taken from the onset of Reconstruction to the continuous assault against prophetic ministry is apparently guided by grace. Former "invisible institutions" that are now cathedrals, schools, and family life centers were erected by the Unseen Mover who created opportunities and generated monies for the emancipation of God's people. This faith forms itself into a belief and adherence to doctrinal and moral truths, a trust that God is on the side of the oppressed, and will not fail them, and a hope that current struggles and misfortunes are not final. To reach a set destination as a people is challenging as many voices have the proclivity to drown out the vision; but faith in the God that is for the betterment of a people as opposed to an individual brings solidarity among the masses. It is in this faith and not individual wills that the Black Church has survived.

---

[95] Albert A. Goodson. "We've Come This Far by Faith," in *African American Heritage Hymnal*, ed. Delores Carpenter and Nolan E. Williams Jr. (Chicago: GIA Publications, 2001), 412.

7th SUNDAY
Baptism

He picked me up, turned me around,
and placed my feet on much higher ground.[96]

To be picked up is to be taken by the hand and lifted upward. This spiritual and anthropological turnaround of one's life is a witness to God's sovereign transformative power. The actual elevation of one's existence and placement into a more stable environment are attributed to a gracious God that orchestrates what the recipient of grace is unable to do for his or herself. God's love lifts the most joyless soul and gives him or her a greater sense of value and purpose for being. This higher ground also has military significance as it reflects a fortress of security as the believers' new place of refuge protects them from their enemies. This personal assemblage of where one was and where one now stands also details the transformative process as one of providential repositioning. To turn away from or repent is a self-willed and desired human response that we lack at times. This text suggests that God is able to transport sinners to places they did not set out to go, but God found favorable for their lives. This act of grace is divinely influenced penitence whereby the sinner or even the oppressed are sometimes carried to higher ground because of their lack of motivation, direction, opportunity, self-love, imagination, or resources.

---

[96] Johnson Oatman Jr. "Holy Ground," in *African American Heritage Hymnal*, ed. Delores Carpenter and Nolan E. Williams Jr. (Chicago: GIA Publications, 2001), 419.

8th SUNDAY

The Civil Rights Movement

We shall overcome.[97]

This determined pursuit of total equality and ancestral belief that the community of the oppressed will one day experience a better day forged itself forward in this tune during the Civil Rights Movement and still resonates within Black Preaching and liturgical singing today. To overcome is to get the better of social, personal, economic, and religious sin. The overcoming of the treacherous and cold hand of racism, sexism, and religious expression is fueled by faith. Although policies, legislative statutes, and constitutional laws may serve as weapons in slaying the oppressive vises that unshamelessly terrorize and subjugate a minority people, it is the faith in the form of vivid images of future freedom that accelerates the pursuit.

This canonized cry is communal in that it is a declaration that all (we) shall be free someday. Total freedom is when all is free. The naming of freedom's day as "someday" connotes an anticipation for each morning to be the potential day of racial atonement. Someday, is before never, and it is a day that God has predestined. No one knows the time when the bell of freedom will ring as to signal an end to oppressive regimes or the abolishment of one's own enslavement to personal and cultural sin, but it can be heard at a distance through the ear of faith.

---

[97] Nolan Williams. "We Shall Overcome," in *African American Heritage Hymnal,* ed. Delores Carpenter and Nolan E. Williams Jr. (Chicago: GIA Publications, 2001), 542.

9th SUNDAY

Rites of Passage for Youth

If you take one step, God will take two.

This implies that there is a transformative anthropological factor to liberation, in that humanity as bearers of God's image and co-creative in nature must partner with God in the meeting of their needs. This appeal to dance with God suggests that through one's faithful effort and usefulness, God will amplify the believer's input. To take one step is progression, but God's response to a believer's faithfulness and desire for change surpasses one's best attempt. God expects the believer to lead in faith as divinity stands at the cross section of faith and practice. This participatory waiting on God to intervene meets grace along the journey; therefore, shortening the wait. When the believer takes one step or claims some responsibility in his or her transformation or prayer request, expectation and hope is more readily realized as the investment one makes in faith is multiplied in God's favor. This utterance refers to both the seeking of salvation and the pursuit of God's will for one's life.

A young lady dreamed of becoming the first college graduate of her family with the ultimate hope of practicing law as a career. After her second year of study she was confronted with the financial woes of dream making as the unexpected death of her uninsured father and skyrocketing college costs decimated her tuition assistance and profoundly compromised her once popular social life. In response she took an additional step of faith by working as a fulltime aid at an area convalescent center. It was at this nursing home that she cared for an aging and childless former attorney who was inspired by her faithfulness and voluntarily paid for her remaining tuition.

10th SUNDAY

Hunger Awareness

The Lord will make a way somehow.

In some unspecified manner or by some unspecified means, God creates paths to better opportunities. There is an uncertainty of how things will improve within one's life when facing a dead-end, but a believer's trusting in God will examine the landscape of the dreaded situation and ultimately embrace the help or escape that God unexpectedly provides. Grace has no shape or color, it just happens. God uses the least likely persons and avenues in order to render salvation unto God's children. This hope that God will make a way keeps one in pursuit of a more excellent but not necessarily plausible reality while maintaining one's sanity when it appears on the surface that the walls are closing in. Not knowing how God will exercise divinity causes the believer not to rule out any possibility.

Somehow is an assurance of unlimited possibilities. The attractiveness of faith is that there are no particularities to that which it seeks. When hard pressed for a positive outcome that contradicts one's current ordeal, one believes that the Lord will deliver; therefore, he or she is attentive and receptive to all potentially favorable results as opposed to an expectation of preferable hence limited means of escape.

11th SUNDAY

A Call to Fast

He's my all and all.

Everything that one needs is supplied for and made possible by God. The tangibility of God is in becoming whatever the believer needs. This monotheistic God is celebrated as immutable but yet flexible in the manifestation of need-specific grace. This sacramental imaginative view accepts God's demonstration of goodness through all forms of creative realities and relationships to provide exactly what the believer needs. The all that God is, is a credit to the full extent that God will go as an expression of God's love for humanity. God is the subtotal of all creation with infinite measures of accessibility and creative form.

If grace is considered to be in all formed creation as well as existence, then God as Creator and Existence supplies unto the believer everything that he or she needs. One's appetite for an authentic friendship is filled in developing a more intimate relationship with Jesus that is consistent with the studying and trusting in His words and actions as a model for one's own life. One can sacrifice unrewarding and inequitable relationships knowing that the Lord lovingly fills the void of loneliness.

12th SUNDAY
Clergy Appreciation

He's a prop on every side.

God as prop is both an invisible and tangible support placed beneath or against the floundering believer to keep him or her from falling. One is made able to stand firm because of the solid and unyielding truth of God's word. The beauty of God's benevolent nature is that it is omnipresent (every side) and made visible in the totality of one's life. The sacrament of living grace is a wholly humanistic virtue of God as a believer is sustained in the professional and relational arena as well as each developmental stage of his or her life. There is nowhere that God is not found in the life of a believer.

Clergy persons who genuinely care for the souls of others carry a double-burden. Home life and concerns run parallel and often times collide with church and community life. This "twoness" is inseparable but requires individual attention that cannot be shared. God cares for and sustains both the personal and professional lives of faithful servants by manifesting grace on both sides. The person who once wrestled with a stress related illness from ministry and a financial crisis in home life can declare that God was there in both situations and used the strength of home to paradoxically help heal church relationships, and equally exercised grace through ministry to alleviate the former struggles in the management of one's own dwelling.

13th SUNDAY
Marriage in Christ

The grass is not always greener on the other side.[98]

Humanity has the inescapable propensity to long for and seek to obtain what others have worked for or inherited justly or even unfairly. The other side is where one is not or what one does not possess but craves for because of misappropriated perception. Believing that others are more significant than self or the one that God has blessed you with is an abomination unto the God of all creation. Relationally, many relationships have been severed because of one's tendency to compare and measure his or her context of living to others. Husbands and wives have stripped their marriages of trust and the once playful courtship because of their constant contrasting of other marriages to their own, or in fact vows were broken as adulterous activity was directly related to the assumption that another could make one's life more satisfying. Experienced believers are able to encourage others to appreciate the blessedness of God in their own lives because of their former taking for granted treasured gifts from God.

As the seasons change, grass withers, fades, or is cut. Each person's life is subject to hidden trials, including those that some model or perceive as ideal. The focus on other persons' treasures shadows the development and prospering of one's own life, while in reality the other's life may not be as substantive and joyful as one may be led to think.

---

[98] Spoken by many but considered to be coined by American author and Unitarian clergyman Robert Fulghum (1937 -).

14th SUNDAY
Triumphant Entry (Palm Sunday)

He'll make a way out of no way.

God will birth modes of deliverance for the demoralized when by all measures it appears as if the doors of relief are shut. To make a way is to obtain an end that is pleasing and contrary to the beginning. God as eternal youth springs forth newness each morning. The omnipotence of God deconstructs the boxes that persons have been placed in and left to shrink into submission. Divinity highlights the unseen lines that lead to a more productive place that has no end. To curtail one's growth is to fashion an environment where development is not encouraged or made available. The believer attests to a God who gives rise to and induces both front and backdoor opportunities of freedom. The typical entry into profitable and more promising lands of opportunity or the exit from tyrannical surroundings are sometimes barricaded by a dominant majority that seeks to maintain unjust equilibrium by keeping a so-called privileged class in and others out. In response God creatively explodes or in some cases implodes the walls of restraint and totalitarian control, thusly, creating newly established avenues of freedom and equal opportunity.

Like a seed that is deeply planted in the ground, God allows rain and wind to part the earth as the budding roots sliver their way through crevices of soil toward the light of day. That which was cast down into surrounding and non-oxygenated darkness was provided a way to the surface of fruitful living. God demonstrates this escape for God's children. There is a way out to everything that has been boxed or caged in.

HOLY WEEK
Good Friday

God will not put more on you than you can bear.

The Christian journey is not impartial to suffering. Impassibility is not a human attribute. The possibilities of pain or of being tormented by external influences are not celebrated by the believer, but they do challenge the believer to take on the cross of Christ. The limitedness of humanity distinguishes human creation from divinity. The frailty of humanness is that it does not possess the capacity to contain all knowledge or remedy all pains. To the believer this is not a flaw but a reason for faith and devotion unto an all powerful and merciful God. God who is capable of bearing all things chooses to handle and take on the burdens of God's children. This atoning act of God redeems the burden bearer of his or her sinful load.

God passionately knows each person's weight load and tolerance for pain. God graciously responds by not exceeding one's breaking point or place of no return. God feels the hurts of humanity, sees the trembling limbs of a burdened down believer, and can measure how much more one can carry, and without deliberation, God keeps further trouble from falling upon the shoulders of God's child. Whatever else that besets an already weakened believer is endured, knowing that Christ is bearing it with him or her.

15ᵗʰ SUNDAY

Resurrection Sunday (Easter)

He got up early *Sunday morning.*

The resurrection of Jesus is celebrated beyond measure in the Black Church as it attests to God's liberating love for the downtrodden. The *getting up* Sunday morning is accentuated with the adverb *early* to connote the coming into being and mysterious dawning of a new day of freedom that is not to be contributed to anyone but God. The earliness of Christ's resurrection is the bridge between death and new life. This period stands between the past (Judeo) and present (Christian) experiences with the building upon the former in order to construct a more promising tomorrow. Jesus' early rising is experienced but not fully captured. Believers therefore communally worship early Sunday mornings as a testament to the Lord's Day and a new first day of the week. Although Sunday is a day of rest and worship to the Black Church, it is also a day of great anticipation as new energies are revived for the forthcoming week. Early on the Lord's Day, soulful celebration is associated with this holy utterance as the reflective lifting and rising of Jesus gives hope that African Americans can also rise from the ashes and take on a new form and revitalized presence in the greater community. Early Sunday morning is the genesis of a new creation; a beginning that is determined by God only. Individuals can recall persons' downfall or death but their date of resurrection is usually unidentifiable because it's a divine act. The early, is a present statement of a retroactive assessment of time that suggests an invisible and unseen movement of God that did not require human influence or approval when it happened. For a sample sermon outline (See Appendix B).

16th SUNDAY

Pentecost Sunday

This joy that I have, the world did not give it to me
and the world cannot take it away.

The internal delight and happiness that is given by God upon one's acceptance of God in his or her life is a priceless endowment. Joy is the gratuitous expression of unmerited favor. Inner joyfulness that is unseen by the world but felt by the believer is graced by God. The baptism of the Holy Spirit deposits internal glee and in return is joyfully expressed as a witness to a hidden but yet visible gift from God that is not subject to carnal expulsion. Although its genuineness is often times questioned and critiqued by a cynical humanity, the world cannot evict joy from the life of one who is spirit filled and refuse to let it go because of his or her remembrance of how life use to be without it.

The world and its secular cultural offerings cannot implant the grace of peace and joy within the hearts of believers. This true form of God's presence in the believer's life is obviously generated by a divine source and is nonrefundable. Americanism and popular culture as ever-evolving pillars of society give, but in return they tax and repossess one's monies, property, and career. Joy has no publicly invested ownership but belongs solely to each believing proprietor who has received it through his or her faith in God. Faith is the deed to joy, a trust that is sealed within the vault of a believer's heart.

17ᵗʰ SUNDAY

Black Women

Can't nobody do me like Jesus.[99]

The friendship of Christ surpasses all relationships in that Christ's fidelity and love is unconditional. Christ meets the needs and performs works within and for the beloved that are without parallel to other persons or authorities. When entering a new relationship, one typically asks "Is he or she genuine?" or "What's in it for me?" With Christ, however, the faithful believes that Christ's primary motive of friendship is to simply be an abiding, loving, nonjudgmental, and supportive presence. The adoption into the fictive family of Christ offers full disclosure and unlimited benefits in Jesus. Others may offer material wealth and even presence, but solidarity, peace, and hope come from Jesus.

A person, who is single, for instance, knows that to be in relationship with Jesus is to be made over again without condemnation, affirmed in true love, and strengthened without chastisement. The love of Jesus is unlike *eros* or *philia* love, for it unconditionally cares for, holdens, protects, and meets the needs of the beloved without rendering a receipt or expecting anything in return. Jesus does something for us that is not necessarily revealed in deed or material gain, but resonates within and enlivens the once forgotten, mistreated, or abused soul.

---

[99] Andraé Crouch, "Can't Nobody Do Me Like Jesus" in *African American Heritage Hymnal*, ed. Delores Carpenter and Nolan E. Williams Jr. (Chicago: GIA Publications, 2001), 384.

18th Sunday

Black Mothers

He's a lawyer in the courtroom.

A lawyer defends or represents clients who are underrepresented. When one is without a voice, God speaks for him or her in a just tone of mercy with the intent to either absolve a transgression or see to it that the punishment fits the crime. Judgment is forever being rendered unjustly toward African Americans and African American boys in particular. According to St. Augustine, as reiterated in Martin King's letter from the Birmingham jail, "An unjust law is in fact no law at all."[100] God, realizing the stereotypical guilt that is place upon the shoulders of minorities responds by making courtroom appearances. Mothers find solace in a faith that God judicially intervenes and will be fair in verdicts. God moves upon the hearts of judges and jurors when a believer is standing before his or her accusers in the court of law and court of public opinion. God is no prejudicial and bifurcated council, but God is the Great Counselor. Many families are unable to afford notable defense teams and must settle with public defenders who carelessly handle the cases of less prominent persons. God however presides every proceeding and for the mother whose son's time was shortened or was completely exonerated; she can attest that God is an advocate of judiciary equality. This divine defense is also revealed in the public domain and counters the cynical societal analysis, guilt, and prejudicial judgment that are placed upon God's people.

---

[100] This is a statement made by St. Augustine and quoted by Martin Luther King, Jr. in his letter from the Birmingham jail.

19th SUNDAY
Men's Day

Please be patient with me,
for God is not through with me yet. [101]

Creation and more specifically humanity are in the process of becoming and developing more completely. Patience is imperative when assessing someone's development and Christian journey. Improvement should be witnessed daily, but measured progressions are according to God's standards. So often the community of faith is in such a haste to see the fruits of a new convert's life that a rush to judgment of one's faithfulness is also accompanied with the right-hand-of-fellowship. God is shaping a believer's life through the evolution of experience. There is a tendency within the church to consider each failed step as finality while discounting a person's discipleship because of past and sometimes current struggles. God on the other hand is perfecting humanity step by step. Just as an unborn fetus goes through three trimesters for a total of nine months of prenatal development before birth, patience is crucial during a believer's early stages of faith as he or she searches for authentic existence. This existential dilemma argues in Aristotelian fervor with the one who judges, that although he or she exists in new life, his or her essence is to be discovered. God is continuously unraveling the mystery of each person's existence while being merciful during the sometimes gradual self-fulfillment.

---

[101] James Cleveland and Albertina Walker. "Please Be Patient With Me." Savagos Music Inc., 1980.

20th SUNDAY
Memorial Day

Jesus paid it all, all to Him I owe.[102]

To thrive within a capitalist society one must have assets, credit, or a reputable name in order to purchase what he or she desires. Material cravings that are plastered on billboards and television ads create an appetite to possess and pay large amounts of money in order to claim possession. There are some things that are for sale, but have actually been paid by the blood of Jesus. Freedom and religious liberties are threatened daily in distant countries, as well as in subtle and diverse ways within our own country. Persons who have been found guilty of both major and minor crimes and transgressions within the body of faith are constantly asked to pay the price or forever suffer public distain. The child of God knows with fervent certainty that these attempts to further tax God's people are unequal to God's pardon of grace.

Although the price has been paid, God only expects witnessing in return by worshipping God and forgiving others as each person has been forgiven. Those who accept the salvation of the Lord believe that the tab has been paid; therefore, just as joy is free, all debt is to be swallowed by the grace of forgetfulness. To have been paid for by Christ or to have had one's debt eradicated through His sacrificial expression of love causes one to worship the giver as well as extend the grace of pardon to others who may be indebted to us.

---

[102] Elvina M Hall, "Jesus Paid It All" in *African American Heritage Hymnal*, ed. Delores Carpenter and Nolan E. Williams Jr. (Chicago: GIA Publications, 2001), 357.

21st SUNDAY

Holy Communion (The Lord's Supper)

He didn't have to do it,
but He did.

Jesus freely offered himself unto fallen humanity as an atoning sacrifice. Free will and heightened individualism have abolished the obligation for even family members to be one another's keeper. God however is constantly offering Godself and the essentials of life to humanity without receipt or a dreaded fear of having to answer to another. Grace is undeserved, unwarranted, and unearned goodness that God extends to a humanity that has done nothing for God.

A young man who in former years voluntarily disbanded himself from his father's house by choosing a life of crime was shot and critically wounded. The young man's wounds led to the discovery that he was born with one kidney and the other was failing because of the bullets vicious path of internal destruction. Hemodialysis treatments were a sustaining treatment but in order to live a fully functional and productive life a kidney transplant was the ideal remedy. The young man's father whom he had fought and disappointed by choosing the streets over a loving home voluntarily offered one of his kidneys to this prodigal son. During his recovery, the young man told those at his beside, "All that I put him through, and all of the hurt I caused him, he didn't have to do it, but he did." This is how the believer reverently witnesses to God's saving grace in his or her life. God delivered and restored many although they did not deserve or earn such acts of kindness.

22nd SUNDAY
Our Elders

He allowed my golden moments
to roll on a little while longer.

Golden moments are a period of peace, prosperous living, and happiness that are attributed to God's grace. Long life is not promised; each day is an allowance given by God to prepare one's heart for eternity. Elders of the faith have discovered their life's calling during the golden years as they were kept just long enough to fulfill their life's purpose. Salutations and praises are given by the one who recognizes that it is the gracious hand of God upon his or her life that has allowed generations to pass before him or her. These treasured moments and memories of God's fidelity indicate generational grace as mothers and fathers are needed to carry on the traditions of faith. Without longevity, traditions would fall into the abyss of generational disconnection.

The elongation of life is to the believer an assertion from God that one has been faithful, one still has ministry to fulfill, and that there is to be a passing on of valued experiences and traditions to the more youthful generations. No one knows how much longer the wheels of life will continue to roll, but as they continue to pass through one day to the next, seasoned saints are internally impelled to assert this pronouncement of favor from God knowing that their lives still have value and purpose.

23rd SUNDAY

Black Children

Everything that looks good to you
ain't necessarily good for you.

Children have a tendency to become fascinated with external aesthetic appeal and beauty. The images that are forced upon young people create an appetite to possess the so called finer things of life. The viewing public places more value on what it sees as opposed to what it hears. Looks and fashion are captivating but oftentimes are used by predators to camouflage agents of death. Discernment is required in order to detect true beauty from veiled ugliness. Addictive substances, such as alcohol, tobacco, and dietary and weight loss supplements, are packaged in appealing wrappings but are potentially deadly.

Persons have entered into and remained in abusive relationships primarily because of a physical attraction. That which is truly good supports, advances, and loves back the beloved. Anything otherwise is not good. Visually pleasing constructs may possess external appeal but may very well be detrimental for one's livelihood. Bad things sometimes adorn themselves in culturally enticing vestments and personalities as in popular culture and liturgical practices. Grace is beautiful even when it is not aesthetically pleasing; however, believers must be aware.

24th SUNDAY
Father's Day

He's God all by Himself.

The monotheistic view of God demonstrates the oneness and sovereignty of God. God does not require assistance in creation or judgment. Gender suspended, God is like mother, father, sibling, judge and jury in that God can call into being and rule without the aid or partnership of others. When a salvific moment is needed and requested by a believer, a believer trusts in the mercy of God instead of an assembly of finite arbitrators. The hope that God reigns supreme and is the one and only Creator and judge rids one of the endless pursuit and fear of pleasing others. Nations have been oppressed for centuries because of the distorted notion that God was operative in the likes of bigoted world leaders. Grace is not generated from the sinfulness of human experience but comes from God and does not need the input of a racist, sexist, and prejudicial humankind. God loves, rules, and judges alone. Much like the devoted and loving fathers of old as it is with mothers of single parent homes who anchor the family in devotion, provide housing, clothing, food, and instruction to their children, and sleep lightly as protector throughout the night—so is God on a cosmic scale. Although God employs agents of divine activity, God is all in one and is able to supply all needs and exercise every power of the godhead alone; for this God is sought above all others.

25ᵗʰ SUNDAY
Urban Ministry

The Lord helps those who help themselves.

This existential appeal invites every believer to be innovative and co-creative with God in the advancement of one's own life. Self and community development are responsibilities of each person. Complaints of injustices are real and warranted in order to bring attention to shadowed truth; complaints is however no excuse for not mobilizing the masses for the betterment of our crime ridden communities. In addition, the pilgrimage toward a more productive and meaningful life also calls for an introspective assessment and declaration to challenge oneself. God provides for those who are without, but one's blessing can be expeditiously realized when he or she engages in the process of created opportunity and personal salvation. The penitent deployment of self anticipates a miracle by becoming a miracle. The one, who longs to escape his or her floundering present reality and dare to take on a new profession or live out a childhood dream, must put faith into praxis. This is done by enrolling into a training program, night school, or working in the field of interest even at an entry level for the necessary experience. God expects humanity to challenge itself and invest in its own progression. It is impossible to prosper and experience good growth without God or the following of God's statutes for kingdom-like living; but the hopeful and positive end result is advanced when we walk in faith and creatively build our own bridges to a better tomorrow. Partnering with God in faith shows forth faithfulness unto God as God blesses those who project a desire to prosper.

93

26th SUNDAY

Nation Building (Fourth of July)

Every day will be like Sunday,
and Sabbath will have no end.

Sunday—the day of resurrection—is also distinguished as the day of both rest and worship within the Black Christian Church. This time of respite provides opportunity to gather oneself after a strenuous work week. Sundays are weekly retreats as well as the premier day of worship. Unlike the laborious Monday through Saturday days of the week where one is often times underpaid, overextended, and unappreciated, Sundays are to be peaceful interludes. It is the Black Church's eschatological hope that there is a perpetual reality after this arduous life that is both the last day of the old life and first day of eternity. God's ideal world is viewed as an everlastingly sabbatical with high praise and worship unto God. This realm of living is a contradiction to the troublesome days of an oppressed people as they lean toward the possibility of being awarded freedom from labor, persecution, and earthly judgment. Sundays in particular will be endless. Sundays are days of personal and communal renewal and rest, unapologetic and unscripted reverence of God, the revealing of life's perplexing mysteries, freedom from the state, authentic kinship, joyful and expressive celebration, equality where everybody is somebody, and empty graves. When the Nation of Eternity is prepared for such a highly anticipating and faithful Diaspora of heavenly oriented people, it shall last forever.

27th SUNDAY
Black Sacred Music

Amazing grace how sweet the sound
that saved a wretch like me.[103]

This grace referenced by John Newton has distinctive meaning to the Black Church. This wondrous favor from God astonished the recipient who at one point felt unworthy of salvation. The salvation attested in this holy saying transcends personal sin, characterized by acts of immorality, and honors God for delivering one from the socially institutionalized sins of the world, such as racism. This sweet sound of the Word of God resonates in the heart of a born-again believer as does the sounding of the freedom bell. This word of salvation is pleasant to the ears of one's soul and is passionately shouted so that others can be made aware of its availability.

The personal wretchedness that one is too readily to claim is often stereotypically cast upon him or her by bigots and those who desire to master over another. Moreover, persons have developed into miserable and unhappy individuals who live lives of degradation until hearing of God's saving grace and love for all humanity. This sound that was transmitted through liberating preaching and singing opened the eyes of the once hopeless and disenfranchised and led them back to more secure surroundings.

---

[103] John Newton, "Amazing Grace" in *African American Heritage Hymnal*, ed. Delores Carpenter and Nolan E. Williams Jr. (Chicago: GIA Publications, 2001), 271.

28th SUNDAY

Black Family

A family that prays together stays together.

A praying family is a functional analogy of God's eternal kingdom. The triune composition of both parents and children with their own uniqueness showcases a paradoxical oneness that is a glimpse of heaven's love, commitment, and diversity. However a family is not constituted in the nuclear sense but is defined more so as a group of persons sharing the same ancestry and common values. A devotional and prayerful family is grounded in the Word of God and in humility that keeps equality between spouses and siblings. Coming together in adoration of a God that is ultimately the Head of the house leads to an appreciation of one another—each who is less than God. As relational beings, believers are held accountable for one another and must earnestly pray for the well being of others. This should be exemplified in the family. A family that takes time out to pray for one another is a family that cares about its well being and future. Attentiveness to the areas of improvement precedes improvement. This prayer is manifested in praying through situations together, as well as in worshipping together, dining with one another, and general table talk where one's true inner self is given the opportunity to be voiced. Prayer is the glue that keeps family members growing in concert with one another.

29th SUNDAY
Christian Education

He's a heart fixer and mind regulator.

Physiologically, the heart is obviously a central organ in the maintenance of living. One cannot live without a heart. The heart is the source and dispenser of life's sustaining blood supply. In the same manner, the mind is an abstract dimension of human comprehension and rationality. The mind is the center of one's consciousness. The believer acknowledges God as a fixer of hearts and regulator of minds, both physically and allegorically. The heart is also the hub of feelings, cares, and desires. Love and forgiveness are products of a heart that has been made right by God. God is capable of changing the hearts of once unbelieving and unforgiving persons. The love of Christ that enters a believer's heart rids it of hatred, envy, and other sins of the heart. The mind of Christ also enters the believer and takes over the thought and thinking process of the old self. The believer who asserts that his or her mind is being regulated or controlled by God is saying that as one who has been recreated in the image of God, "I am a rational and imaginative being whose outlook is pure positivity." That which was once broken or distorted has been put back together by God and filled with compassion, hope, and sound mindedness.

30ᵗʰ SUNDAY
Black Martyrs

Without struggle there is no progress.[104]

Frederick Douglas's fervent words have entered into the canon of the Black Church because of the church's theological view that cross bearing is an inherent course towards progress. Brokenness oftentimes precedes blessedness. Freedom is not free and calls for sacrifice. Progress is an attempt to escape mediocrity, and whenever the status quo is challenged the stabilizing factors that have kept one at bay will resist. Cross bearing will bring about protest from those who oppose freedom for all. This cross' honor is heightened however with each slashing it takes. The more ridicule, the more righteous it becomes. The advancement of a once enslaved people is confronted with its own internal strife as the Willie Lynch syndrome causes a crab-like atmosphere that detests the progression of its own people.

This struggle is also internal as the new self pulls away from the old self. Much like the birth of a child and the separation between the placenta and uterine wall, a rupture must take place in order to bring forth new life. The progress of a subjugated people and the Black Church specifically is virtually impossible without stages of struggle. Good growth guarantees confrontation, but it is nevertheless celebrated as confirmation of liberating progression.

---

[104] Reginald McKnight, *African American Wisdom*, (Novato: New World, 2000), 109. This holy saying was originally delivered by Frederick Douglas in 1857, as quoted from a larger discourse on the price of freedom.

31st SUNDAY
Racial Reconciliation

Blessed assurance Jesus is mine,
O what a foretaste of glory divine. [105]

Blessed assurance is an absolute confidence that the Christ has come unto humanity. The incarnation of God in Jesus has established within the believer's heart that Jesus' life demonstrates how one ought to live, but He has also shown the believer that the region of pure Godhead is eternal. The historical Jesus who lived was able to overcome that which He was subjected to and then come again unto believers in Spirit to show the reality of eternity. The foretaste of glory is the example, preview, and sample of Jesus' living presence which symbolizes something greater to come. The hope to see Jesus and to be in God's everlasting presence is birthed out of the sneak preview of God in the historical and proclaimed life of Jesus. The faith of the believer allows him or her to imaginatively see a better future and world as well as celebrate the glorious times of today. Living in Christ and knowing that Christ resides within substantiates one's existence as it borrows from an already created but not yet realized world where the believer will see the fullness of God. This is the storyline for all of those who claim to be reconciled unto God through the acceptance of Jesus as Lord.

---

[105] Fanny J. Crosby (1820-1915), "Blessed Assurance, Jesus is Mine," *African American Heritage Hymnal*, 508.

32nd SUNDAY

An Awesome God

He's alright (Ain't He Alright, I know He's Alright).

Nuanced in various syntaxes of the black religious vernacular, this exclamatory statement is a pronouncement that God is all together good. The grandeur and wonderful offerings of Godself to the believing community leads one to be hard pressed to articulate one's gratefulness to God. Over and above the constant unfolding of new experiences whereby God creatively delivers grace unto an undeserving humanity, what else can be said about this gracious God? This is not to suggest that we have narrowed God down to mere words, but in fact that it is impossible to use broken, fallible, and common words to define divinity. The colorful and metaphorical marriages between words create a tension and paradox that references a reality much greater than ourselves, but we still fall short in description.

This "lastly but not least" exuberant and celebratory expression of faith is an exclamation to the majesty of God and the mysterious movement of God that has been realized in a believer's life. Other persons, institutions, and powers may be acceptable and satisfactory in their deportment and care for others, but to the believer God is better than the greatest calculation or conceivable notion of goodness. Nothing else can or needs to be said except God is alright—absolutely good.

33rd SUNDAY
Black Scientists and Inventors

I know the Lord will fix it after while.

This faith statement is a belief that God will alter, change, or make better a situation in reasonable time. Once one accepts that his or her efforts, knowledge, resources, or influence cannot solve or determine a desirable outcome, full-time and unseen faith is activated. Not knowing or having a point of reference to how matters will be resolved can lead to chronic worrying. A knowing that is based on past experiences enlivens the believer by causing him or her to stop worrying and trust that God will exercise God's omnipotence as a means to correct what is unfixable with human faculties. When it is highly unlikely that a stress will be alleviated by even a believer's best and most resolute effort, one must eventually lay his or her brokenness before the altar and trust that the Potter will put him or her back together again.

A loving wife begged of her husband on countless occasions to secure one of the kitchen table chairs before it would collapse beneath someone. The legs were being pried apart from its seating. It was rarely in use as the children had now moved on and visited only on holidays. To the wife's surprise, her mother and a few of her friends unexpectedly stopped by one morning. Before she could redirect one of the ladies to another seating the guest sat down in the chair that she assumed had not been fixed. To her astonishment it held the weight of her guest. The husband had heard his wife's complaint and had fixed the chair weeks ago when he had time to nail and re-glue each stud. God does not necessary fix things when we initially request of them or when they have been broken, but God fixes them when we need them the most.

34th SUNDAY
Homegoing Celebration (Funeral)

There's a bright side somewhere.[106]

There is a place that believers turn to when all else has failed and it appears as if everything that is around them is insufficient and utter darkness. The believer turns toward an invisible elsewhere. There is no more darkness in the Brightside which is somewhere other than one's current residency. The deliverance of God may require movement or a relocating to a place of peace and refuge. The Brightside does not suggest a time, but a location. The Brightside is locatable. Although there is an obvious heavenly overtone, there are places outside of one's current condition of existence and *sitz em leben* that are more suitable for one's survival. Freedom is sometimes found in a foreign land and requires a leaving of familiarity in order to escape the darkness. This place is not mapped out nor is its distance or time of travel known, but it is out there somewhere. The expedition toward somewhere requires an opening of one's eyes in faith and sojourning toward a new land of recovered sight and hospitality. Death is sometimes viewed as the path that one must take in order to reach the land that is free from suffering, pain, and loneliness. On the contrary, for those who grieve after the departure of a love one, the preacher often points them to a beloved Brightside that will shine light even upon the darkness of death.

---

[106] Delores Carpenter & Nolan E. Williams, eds., "There's a Bright Side Somewhere," in *African American Heritage Hymnal* (Chicago: GIA Publications, 2001), 411. The hymn "There's a Bright Side Somewhere" is from an anonymous source but has been echoed throughout the hollowed walls of countless Black Churches.

35th SUNDAY

Education Day (Back to School)

God is good, all the time, and all the time, God is good.

This collective call-and-response of God's immeasurable goodness is an indication that it is infinite. There is no break or end to God's righteousness. Communally, believers attest to the God of timeless grace by this choral witnessing of God and this epikletic call for God's presence. The invoking of an already existing presence is pronounced when God's benevolent virtue is needed or has been manifested in the life of a faith community. Grace as time demonstrates how the God of existence and potentiality is always at hand. God is never bad or less than generous. This perpetual graciousness of God is pronounced both in times of struggle and times of security. The absoluteness of God's nature as being totally good is derived from one's favorable encounters with God. The good that God is proclaimed as being is both virtue and essence. If God was to stop being good, then God would cease to be. Being that God is good, all that God does is pleasing. God cannot escape Godself, for God is eternal.

36th SUNDAY
Labor Day

O what a friend we have in Jesus. [107]

A friend in Jesus is a confidant and companion throughout all times and one who both corrects and reassures the beloved. True friendship does not sugarcoat the truth about one's less than virtuous lifestyle nor does it stop loving the beloved once a moral sin has been committed. In fact, Jesus as friend expresses a greater desire to be with the one who has fallen. Often times it is hard to find an acquaintance such as this that has unbiased motives and is willing to mutually share his or herself with the other. Characterized by confidentiality and a non-condemning character, Jesus finds joy in being in relationship with His beloved brothers and sisters. Jesus identifies His disciples as friends and calls each person into service in spite of his or her mistake-ridden life. Abandonment often times leads to a distorted notion that there is no need to repent since love ones have also given up on the transgressor. For this, Jesus goes the extra mile to take care of us and vindicate us by being in relationship with us. To know that your life matters to someone of such honor and high stature is redemptive. The believer is never alone with Jesus as friend. Jesus as friend seeks and chooses the believer as friend. One does not have to bargain or purchase His love; it is free.

---

[107] Joseph M. Scriven (1819-1866), "What a Friend We Have in Jesus," *African American Heritage Hymnal*, 431.

37ᵗʰ SUNDAY
Health and Wellness Day

He's a doctor that never lost a patient.

Death has been the inevitable outcome to many dreaded diseases and sicknesses. One often loses hope when the prognosis is poor or less than assuring. As a consequence, doctors and healthcare providers are looked upon by some as agents of death as opposed to healers. Many old-time saints can recall how persons entered hospitals relatively well to never return again. God, however, is looked upon as a Great Physician and Divine Doctor that chooses to use miracle working power to restore or even prescribe death as a reasonable option and possible cure. God as doctor has never pronounced a patient dead, because as believers they continue to live in God.

A mother of five and faithful wife was lying in her deathbed surrounded by her children and extended family while cancer rapidly ate away at her inside. She began to pray as she reached toward something that could only be seen by her and thanked God for her husband, her children, her church family, and even for healing her. Shortly thereafter, her healing was realized in death. God as doctor did not lose her as a patient, but God healed her as a faithful servant. Believers who trust in God never die but are healed through death. In the mind of the believer, God has never been found guilty of malpractice or the loosing of a child of God to a dreaded disease or sudden trauma. The disease or ailment may kill, but God still keeps. Death is therefore viewed as a constituent of healing.

38th SUNDAY

The Middle Passage (The MAAFA)[108]

He's a bridge over troubled waters. [109]

Bridges are constructs that are built to transport persons over waters or ravines. Bridges are necessary for insuring safety while crossing raging waters, but they are also time efficient and narrow the time it takes to travel from one point to the next. God exists at all points of travel, from the beginning to the end and in between. The universality and "betweenness" of God carries God's children over life's obstacles and valleys. The benefit of being carried over as opposed to through something is that a bridge does not subject you to the potentially deadly elements of furious waters. The invisible hand of God keeps believers from being consumed by drowning waters as they travel across difficulty. God's bridges include mysterious happenings in one's life and also the believer's more intuitive nature and better judgment in the face of surrounding threats. For many believers, bullets have been literally dodged as they were able to miraculously escape from potentially deadly surroundings and led to safety.

---

[108] MAAFA is a Swahili term that means "Great Disaster" and refers to the TransAtlantic Slave Trade that took place between the 16th and 19th centuries.

[109] "Bridge over Troubled Water" was performed by Aretha Franklin but originally composed and sung by Paul Simon and Art Garfunkel in 1969.

39th SUNDAY

Substance Abuse Awareness Day

He's been better to me than I've been to myself.

Alcoholism, substance abuse, and the battered lover syndrome are threats that are not to be taken lightly. Individual proclivities and the human need of affirmation have led countless persons down the dark ally of these addictive behaviors. The child of God must not be a practitioner of his or her own demise. There is a tendency to aid in one's own destruction because of crumbling self-impressions and moderate to low self-esteem. Sin attacks our perception of self-value and whispers words of meaningless existence into our psyche. This evolves into long-term and risky behaviors that can be suicidal. One's acceptance of God's indwelling spirit into his or her life stops the self-mutilation and gives greater reason for living. The knowledge that God has done great things for humanity and loves creation in spite of justifiable guilt causes one to love self back. An acceptance of God's love being greater than any love initially shocks the one who has been a contributor to his or her own demise. This awakening celebrates life and the goodness of God that finds value even in wretchedness. The atoning love of God in Jesus causes a human response that seeks to honor one's own life as much as God has through the sacrifice of Jesus, and through the investment of Godself in the indwelling of the Holy Spirit.

40th SUNDAY

Global Mission Day

If I can help somebody
then my living will not be in vain.[110]

The believer desires to be used by God to bless others. God made humankind in God's image as relational and creative beings. God expects persons to be for one another and to have an undying appetite to aid those in distress. Life intends for us to love humanity regardless of ethnic, racial, or gender differences. To offer self and one's giftedness for the benefit of others is commendable by God's standards of meaningful existence. God is well pleased when we help to make someone's life better by consistently leading them to the gateway of their God oriented potential.

To selfishly watch others stand in great need and do nothing is an abomination and makes one's life null and void. To have done nothing good for anyone is to have not lived at all. Therefore, believers look for opportunities to help others so that their own lives will not be considered wasteful in the Day of Judgment. The conjunction "if" implies chance, a granting of, or opportunity. Believers both inquire about and create opportunities to serve the other so that their own lives will be fulfilled in the sight of God.

---

[110] The hymn "If I Can Help Somebody" was copyrighted by A. Vazel Androzzo in 1945, arranged by Kenneth Morris.

41st SUNDAY

Homecoming

Hold to God's unchanging hand.[111]

God's human creation evolves as it matures and develops from within itself. This evolution of being can also potentially lead to an altering of mind and relation to others that may or may not be virtuous. Transitions are inescapable realities, and consequentially persons can change for the worse. God is however unchangeable. God as mere existence can take shape in any form of expression that God wills to be necessary as well as reveal Godself throughout all ages and subcultures. The believer's conviction is that the pure essence of God is eternal and immutable. This consistent nature of God gives one something that is substantially longstanding and trustworthy. The Black Church holds to the truth of God's Living Word. This dependence upon a just God gives footing and stability to an ever changing world that has the propensity to forget those that choose not to move when the dominant culture says move.

---

[111] Jennie Wilson, "Hold on to God's Unchanging Hand," African American Heritage Hymnal, 104. This idiom of Black Faith has been extracted from the hymn "Hold to God's Unchanging Hand" by Jennie Wilson.

42nd SUNDAY

Revival

I might not be what I ought to be,
but I thank God I'm not what I used to be.

This holy claim of humility and honesty about one's spiritual journey is an actual declaration of thanksgiving for the transformation that God has brought about in the life of the witness. A change has taken place in the life of one who utters these words. If perfection is possible for vulnerable creatures such as us, it is in knowing that true discipleship is a continuous call and process of being perfected unto the image of Christ. The gradual change that is happening in the believer's living is better than where he or she used to be or no change at all. The submission to God's will for one's life can further develop one into a more sanctified person of faith. Following a personal revival experience, one recognizes that although the journey has been marred with moral blunders, his or her life is still stages ahead of where it was.

A forty year old woman who once lived a promiscuous life as a teenager and young adult stood to share her riveting testimony on the third and final night of a high spirited revival. She categorized in shaded fashion some of her past transgressions and how she still wrestled with rocky relationships because of her distrust of men. Although she was never proud of her former actions and admitted to being far from perfection, she attested how thankful she was to God that she is no longer the person she was. Her age was a testament of her maturity, but as a born again believer, she accredited God's transforming and still sculpturing hand as the cause of her change.

43rd SUNDAY
Being Single

*He walks with me and He talks with me
and He tells me that I am His own.* [112]

The believer claims how Jesus accompanies him or her in every facet of life. The presence of Christ during periods of loneliness and isolation from the greater community is affirming to a joyless soul. It is human nature to desire relationship and to be among persons who genuinely care about you. To know that you are a member of God's family and that you belong to the fictive family of faith reassures one's value, voice, and sense of belonging. Conversational prayer reassures the believer that God loves him or her and claims him or her as a father or mother claims a child. God taps into the spirit of man and woman and generates a dialogue between humanity that imaginatively assures persons that God is really concerned and claims ownership to his or her life. This testimonial pronouncement refuels the faith of a believer who has been abandoned by a lover, dechurched by an affiliated congregation, or disbanded from polite society. To know that one is of God eases the hurt feeling that one's life no longer matters to others.

---

[112] C. Austin Miles (1868-1946), "In the Garden," *African American Heritage Hymnal*, 494. This is an excerpt from the choral response in the hymn *"In the Garden."*

44th SUNDAY
Black Colleges

God can do anything but fail.

Failure is falling short of a set goal. It is not quite hitting the mark or achieving a particular standard of excellence. Although humanity is fully capable of achieving great expectations as it transcends beyond itself, it is yet still fallible, therefore failure according to societal standards is possible. Excellency is relative in the narrow sense and almost impossible to achieve, but God is perfect and in God there is no failure. An allegiance to God's will and devotedness to God's statutes can lead to a successful and fulfilling life. God's will is characteristically different from capitalistic principles and popular views of success. In Christ we are all victors, but triumphalism is not indicative of God's will as even suffering can be viewed as conquest as in the case of Jesus' death and subsequent resurrection.

For a believer, anything that is scrutinized as a disappointment may in fact be God's will for his or her life. The end result is not indicative of a meaningless or failing past. Some historical Black colleges and universities have been stricken with financial woes and even closed, but God who erected these institutions of higher learning has not failed in their purpose because many men and women were educated within those walls of academia. If God chooses to foreclose certain opportunities, it is not a failing attempt by a perfect God, but a means to create new direction.

45th SUNDAY
Interfaith Day

Let the church say Amen.

Amen (so let it be) declared within the ecclesial setting and the auspices of preaching is a communal call of affirmation and assent. This "Say that it is so" and "You are right on it" is confirmation to the necessity and "right-now-ness" of the proclaimed Word of God. The listening ear comes to know the value of a remark by the resounding amen in the voices of the witnessing multitude. This compelling and corporate witness of a truth reinforces what has been said by the preacher, prayed by the saint, or sung by the choir. Amen is an acknowledgement of a church's oneness and reverent recognition of a doctrinal observance. The body must be reminded that such a liturgical response is warranted. The church is asked to confirm the goodness of God or the preacher's prophetic consciousness by being called upon to demonstratively declare "amen." To respond in the negative when summoned to agree with a proclaimed biblical or cultural truth is a rebellion against the preacher or sign of inattentiveness. Amen is the exclamation to a sermonic proposition that was expected to convict the listener of his or her wrongdoings, grip the listener's heart of an apparent oversight, or tease them into a particular and necessary action.

46th SUNDAY

Black Literature Day

Can I get a witness?

A witness is one who has observed the loving hand of God upon someone's life or has experienced the power of God in his or her own life. The witness is therefore encouraged to share with others the goodness of God. The witness of God's blessedness is a change agent and living exhibit of God's transforming or delivering power. The credibility of preaching is heightened to a level of sacredness when hearers of this proclaimed truth can attest to its validity in their own lives. This is especially pertinent when statespersons of the church are moved to show the relevance and convincing proposition of the preach word. A preacher's request for a witness is not for self approval or appeasement but for the glorification of a God act. The eyewitnesses and recipients of a blessing are often times solicited by the preacher to substantiate a divine truth by such living witnesses. The imaginative vision and creative genius of the preacher is made more attractive when others can actually confirm its worth. A witness is needed each Sunday to help amplify the voice of the preacher.

A rather silk stocking-like rural church was governed by a family of reputable status. Pastors' tenures and prophetic visions were unfortunately predicated on amicable relationships between them and the pastorate. On one occasion, a member of this dignified and domineering family responded to the pastor's plea for a witness while preaching the saving grace of Jesus Christ. The witness expressed himself in dance and shouting. This led to a breakthrough in the church's stoic history whereby the pastor was reverently viewed as one that could even chip away the ice of one of the coldest hearts.

114

47th SUNDAY

Thanksgiving

Thank you, for putting food on my table
and a roof over my head.

The bare necessities of life are often times taken for granted, particularly when they have never been threatened or interrupted. Food is an essential requirement for survival and worthy of being thankful for. God who is the source of all creation is to be praised for providing food to a hungry humanity. Many homes struggle to offer a well-balanced meal as sky-rocketing food cost has left shelves empty and children malnourished. Thanksgiving is rendered unto God for feeding the children of the world and giving enough to maintain health.

Shelter and security should never be viewed as a guarantee and therefore should be continuously appreciated. There are persons who are without safe havens; yet, those who own homes complain about their square footage or neighborhood. God has not abandoned those who are homeless, for they are still with God. In fact, God has put (placed, positioned, set, situated) the necessities and abundance of life before God's people with the expectation that the believing community will reverently respond to God in praise as well as feed those who are hungry and provide shelter for those who are homeless.

48th SUNDAY

Advent

He's an on time God.[113]

Believers intently wait on predestined and created opportunities because they know that they are revealed in God's perfect timing. The longing for something that is very much a necessity can lead to long nights and shattered faith, but the joy of deliverance is like the breaking of a new day. The blessing that one has stood in need of comes as does the morning. The time of human expectation is in most cases offset from God's time (*kairos*). God displays grace after one has anticipated it, but in the same manner God shows Godself in new ways before believers even realize the need that God has already filled. God who transcends time is independent of time and is not bound by the continuum of set years, days, or minutes. When God's will is executed in visible form, it is the only moment that matters. God is always on time because God is forever present and available through endless and sometimes uncharacteristic means of manifestation. The coming of the Lord and His blessings are precise and preordained; it is our anxiousness and demanding wants that are off schedule.

---

[113] This holy saying is found in the gospel "On Time God" that was composed and performed by Dottie Peoples in 1994.

49th SUNDAY
Stewardship

Have you tried Him?

This resounding inquiry is raised to move one to witness how his or her trust in God has benefited, and at some point made his or her life better. To try Jesus is to test one's faith by being obedient to His call upon one's life and God's written commandments. To try Jesus is to emulate His morality, ethics, and theo-political disposition. To try Jesus is to become a living testimony of a grace and hope-centered life, and a follower of Christ even when it is unpopular. One who cannot respond in the affirmative is not necessarily one who does not believe in the Incarnate and still-living Christ, but is one who may lack confidence in his or her own faith walk—one that needs to be called unto true discipleship.

Like many old timers who were reluctant to visit and follow the medical prescriptions of doctors because of their uncertainty of the physicians' knowledge or their lack of trust in modern medicine, helpful drugs were never tried and consequently pains persisted until death; so much so is it with avid church goers. We must trust and seek the spirit of Christ (which has the tendency to manifests itself in unassuming forms) for ourselves rather than the mere following of tradition or the practicing of grandmother's religion. To try Jesus is to suspend reason and fear and to cast all of one's weight upon a faith that God knows and will do what is best for one's human condition.

50th SUNDAY

Kwanzaa[114]

There's a reason for the season.

Every created reality has a season or time that its true purpose or reason is made evident. Humanity in general and a community's traditional celebrations of former glories, struggles, and feats specifically, all have a season and primary purpose to be celebrated, but they are nevertheless subject to being forgotten. All cultural and religious celebrations have long and meaningful histories but are oftentimes not fully expounded upon or fully recognized. The liturgical season of Christmastide was intended to be a celebratory commemoration of God's presentation of Jesus as the living testament of humanity's true capacity to love, forgive, be joyful, and reign in peace. Kwanzaa's purpose is to celebrate the sacredness of family, community, and culture. Material idolatry and cultural and economic appeasement shadow the true purpose of the season. Gifts are intended to show one's gratefulness for the manifestation of love in one's life. These days of reverent reflection are not to create a greater burden of financial obligation, but to honor love. For this the Black Church is to be reminded.

---

[114] Kwanzaa is an African American holiday beginning on December 26 and ending on January 1. African Americans celebrate their African culture, respectfulness toward community, and love for family. There are seven primary symbols in Kwanzaa with two supplementals that represent values of African culture. They are Mazoa (The Crops), the rewards of productive labor; Mkeka (The Mat), the foundational traditions which we build; Kinara (The Candle Holder), our ancestral roots; Muhindi (The Corn), our children and future as a people; Mishumaa Saba (The Seven Candles), the seven values of African people that are lit on each of the seven day celebration—one black, three red, and three green; Kikombe cha Umoja (The Unity Cup), the practice of unity; Zawadi (The Gifts), the labor and love of parents that are kept by children; Bendera (The Flag), black for the people, red for the struggle, and green for the hopeful future; and the Nguzo Saba Poster (Poster of the Seven Principles).

51st SUNDAY

Christmas

God moves in mysterious ways.

God moves in ways that are unknown, unexpected, and unaccustomed to the status quo. The mystifying movement of God keeps believers looking for the happening of grace in all forms in and through unlikely places and unsuspecting people. The overlooking of this sacramental display of Godself shows how even the believer has the proclivity to box God in by attempting to define divinity and its most appropriate manifestation. The Black Church can account for how God radically changed communities and persons by baffling means and personalities. This is the foolishness of the Gospel in that it is a contradiction to human comprehension and scientific reasoning. This anti-religious statement is a trusting in the newness of God as Eternal Youth, as opposed to the celebrated and even proven traditions of the Faith. Christmas is a time of new appearances, rekindled love, and expressions of gratefulness. These acts are generally surprising; for although highly anticipated or desired, the channel by which God transports grace and the sometimes unappealing package that it comes in is baffling.

The Paschal Mystery is one of unexplainable events and God's empowerment of peculiar personalities. Christmas was fairly cold and lonely for an elderly couple whose only son who lived across country was unable to spend yet another Christmas with them or his own family because of a critical business meeting. That was until his plane was redirected because of severe weather. Just so happened he was only a few hours from his childhood home. His parents considered his surprise visit to be the best gift that they had received in years. Mother simply replied, "God moves in mysterious ways".

52ⁿᵈ SUNDAY
Culmination Celebration

When I look back over my life
and see how good the Lord has been to me.

Every day and every year that comes to a closure must reflect upon the journey and lessons learned throughout the days. Looking back and examining one's life through faith instead of nostalgic remembrance and the regretting of bad choices leads to a celebration over the distance God has brought one. The integrity and faithfulness of God is seen in God's sustaining grace and the many avenues that God paved toward a better outcome in one's life. The anamnetic reflection does memorialize the past as a treasured moment in history but thinking back also invokes a praise dance and exultation to the God of present day reality and future hopes. Remembering and sometimes reminiscing (with great detail) the former years of one's life serve as a launching pad of heightened awareness of God's merciful acts in the believer's life. It is not living in the past, but appreciating and praising God for the present day. The growth and sustaining grace that has brought one thus far is all contributed to God's goodness. God did it for "Me". This testimonial declaration is personal and leads the one who has been kept throughout all of his or her life or as far as he or she can look back, to individually praise God for all of the good that God has done in the life of the redeemed.

DECEMBER 31ST WORSHIP CELEBRATION
Watch Night Service

Put it in God's hands.

The hand of God is a theological viewpoint that God is greater than all being and that both creation and destruction is willed by God. The hand of God can grip one's own hand as well as hold every trouble that one may have. To place or hand over one's problems to God is to confess one's own inability to resolve them and to profess one's faith in a God that will. God's hands extend an invitation to the people of faith to let some things go, as well as to place valued relationships and possessions under the management of God. This turning over of our cares to God allows us to release the burdens of the past and find forgiveness by finally being able to wash our hands of old matters. The purity of God's presence is not tainted by whatever is turned over to God in prayer and a more devoted life; humanity, on the other hand, is given merciful rest by the relinquishing of the burdensome matters that it once carried in its own hands. There is a sense of cosmic security and invisible presence in the placing of one's life into the hands of God. Upon the cross, Jesus surrendered His being into the hands (will) of God.

A rather observant father noticed how his two daughters would instinctively reach out and put their hands into his hands whenever they would pass through an unfamiliar and crowded setting such as a theme park, beach, or mall. It was his belief that they found safety in their father and that their dad would not allow the stranger or predator to harm them. They would be eased in their knowing that their father knew of their apprehensions and that he never shook off their gripping and sometimes sweaty and soiled hands. Their father was made happy because they trusted in him. So much so is God.

121

Appendix A
Sermon

This is Holy Ground

Exodus 3:1-10 NIV

Now Moses was tending the flock of Jethro his father-in-law, the priest of Midian, and he led the flock to the far side of the desert and Horeb, the mountain of God. There the angel of the Lord appeared to him in flames of fire from within a bush. Moses saw that though the bush was on fire it did not burn up. So Moses thought, "I will go over and see this strange sight— why the bush does not burn up." When the Lord saw that he had gone over to look, God called to him from within the bush, "Moses! Moses!" And Moses said, "Here I am." "Do not come any closer," God said. "Take off your sandals, for the place where you are standing is holy ground." Then he said, "I am the God of your father, the God of Abraham, the God of Isaac and the God of Jacob." At this, Moses hid his face, because he was afraid to look at God. The Lord said, "I have indeed seen the misery of my people in Egypt. I have heard them crying out because of their slave drivers, and I am concerned about their suffering. So I have come down to rescue them form the hand of the Egyptians and to bring them up out of that land into a good and spacious land, a land flowing with milk and honey—the home of the Canaanites, Hittites, Amorites, Perizzites, Hivites, and Jebusites. And now the cry of the Israelites has reached me, and I have seen the way the Egyptians are oppressing them. So now, go. I am sending you to Pharaoh to bring my people the Israelites out off Egypt.

Have any of us noticed what is going on in this postmodern world? It appears to me that some of us have become so engulfed and enthralled with the new thing, so influenced by popular culture, and even by the gift of diversity that we have began to embrace any and everything that compliments contemporary society and our own personal fetishes, as absolute truth.

As a result, in the minds of some of us; that which has been longstanding and long lasting has played out and gone out of style. This postmodernist poison has even entered the blood stream of the church. And because of this disease, some persons feel that in order for the church to survive and attract today's world, it must sacrifice its holiness and learn to keep up with culture. Therefore, it is becoming increasingly more difficult to distinguish some churches from the club, some preachers from pimps, and some congregants from wannabe game show contestants—Let's Make a Deal.

Now I know that as the church we must meet the people where they are—we must remain relevant and proactive instead of reactive. But after spending some time with this text and juxtaposing it with our contemporary ecclesial context, I am convinced that some things have been created by God to be and forever remain holy. God has designed some things to be distinctive, unique, and unlike any other created reality. For God moves and reveals Godself in mysterious ways in order to convict us—to challenge us—and commission us. And if we want to continue to hear from God, we must continue to keep some things holy—especially the church.

Here within the Word of God, Moses is found tending to the flock of his father-in-law Jethro in the desert near Horeb. While Moses was in the desert, the angel of the Lord appeared to him in a burning bush, that was not consumed. Moses said let me go over and see why it is that this bush is on fire but does not burn up.

God saw Moses approaching the bush and called him by name. Don't come any closer and take off your sandals, Moses, for you are on holy ground. Kick off and take off that which you have been walking around in and defined by—for you are now on holy ground. So that we don't run the risk of contaminating the sanctuary we must kick off our shoes. For if we were to bring our soiled shoes in here, we may leave thinking that our help was in what we brought with us instead of what God has to offer us. It's not your shoes or my shoes—it's not your experiences or my experiences—it's not your melodious voice or my sonorous preaching, but it's the burning bush—it's God's holiness.

What many of us must learn to do is take our shoes off—uncloak ourselves of our cultural influences and open ourselves up to the holy. The holy will compel you to remove your regalia and your surname, for it may be credible but not necessary. Moses took his sandals off because the stuff that he had been standing on and walking on throughout Horeb did not belong before the burning bush.

The burning bush is sacramental, for it both reveals and conceals God's grace. As Augustine said, it is invisible grace made visible. It shows us just enough and compels us to want to see a little more. Holy things—holy realities—emphasize how God is discoverable here and now but at the same time leads us to yearn for the fullness of our experience of God in eternity.

Moses was both afraid and fascinated. That's what the holy will do. As Rudolf Otto best said it. The holy is both *mysterium tremendum* and *mysterium fascinans*. It terrifies us, yet attracts us. And I look unto the church and even this place—the Grand Hyatt Baptist Church—as being holy. For much like the burning bush it grips us and excites us. It frightens us and it fascinates us.

More specifically, it causes us to acknowledge our weaknesses. Moses approached the burning bush. He approached the bush that was already burning. The bush was burning without the aid and initiative of Moses. God ignited the flame. God created and cared for the bush. The bush existed before and without Moses. In the same manner the church and our rich vernacular of faith were here before we came, and the flame will continue to burn long after we are gone. I have discovered that sometimes our disappointments, frustrations, and let downs are self-afflicted, because we think that we possess the knowledge and will to solve all of life's problems. And when we are unable to control the environment or start the fire, we become depressed and even upset at God. But we must understand that although we may be gifted—we are not God. We might very well create and control things out there—but holy things are handled by God.

We must learn to accept the fact that we may not possess all of the answers—that we are limited; that we are the subject and not the object or center of discussion. In order to hear from God we must engage in complete personal disclosure. We must know who we are and who we are not. We are not the dean of every discipline. We are fallible, fragmented, and frail, but the Good News is that there is a God somewhere—much greater than you and I.

We are fearfully and wonderfully made by God, but we are sub-divine. We have been created in the image of God, but we are not God. We ought to rejoice, however, for in spite of our weaknesses and shortcomings God nevertheless invites us into God's presence. We are still privileged to position ourselves in the presence of the holy, and in doing so we are strengthened. God is the source of our strength and the strength of our lives. God's grace is sufficient. My beloved and departed grandmother had an old wood stove. We would enter into her home, and it seemed as if the wood stove was always burning—from September to April. We did not start the fire; we supposed Grandma started the fire, but we were still recipients of the warmth that it offered. As a matter of fact, we were still privileged to go to the woodpile every now and again and add a few logs to the fire. I'm glad that the woodstove is still burning, and yet in spite of our weaknesses God endears us enough to occasionally add a few sticks to the fire.

The holy also affords us an opportunity to witness the wonders of God. It was burning—on fire—but not consumed. How could this be? It is the happening of grace. It is not supposed to be this way, but it is. The bush should be consumed. But the holy is unlike the unholy or worldly. Styles, fads, rhetoric, and trends play out, but the holy keeps burning. Kevin Irwin reminds us that all reality is potentially or in fact the bearer of God's presence and an instrument of God's saving activity.

Moses was working in the desert, but the bush was provided by God as a diversion and haven of hope. In the same manner the church is that place that harnesses and displays the wonders of God, for in here you are among people who are walking miracles—contradictions to modern medicine and sociological statistics.

You may have had an infectious disease invade your body, but you are not consumed. Someone's son or daughter is addicted to a foreign substance—living in the streets, unemployed, and malnourished—but not consumed. Someone is in financial despair but not consumed. Some churches have over-extended their budgets and members have decided to stop giving, but they are not consumed. The doors are still open.

That's why I love the church, for it is the house of miracles. When you are in God's house something supernatural takes place. The bush was burning but not consumed. What a wonder.

Finally, the holy always offers a word for the weary. Much is being said on television and radio—and some of what is being said is useful; but there is something different about the words of the world and the Holy Word that you receive from the burning bush.

God spoke to Moses through the burning bush—not while tending the sheep or in Jethro's house but through the burning bush. Not from Mt. Sinai or upon two tables of stone, but through the burning bush. God told Moses, "I have seen the afflictions of my people which are in Egypt, and I have heard their cry and know their sorrow—and I have come down to deliver them out of the hands of the Egyptians and to bring them out of that land and into a land filled with milk and honey." And don't be afraid of your Pharaoh, for I am with you. God expressed Godself in the form of the vernacular rhetoric of an oppressed people. God will talk your talk, in order to inform and encourage you.

What a word—a word of assurance—a word of deliverance—a word of providential prosperity—a word for the weak and the weary. Not just for one particular person, but a word for all of God's people— the oppressor and the oppressed—the pimp, pusher, and prostitute.

Street talk and slang changes—but God's Word remains the same. And you can find a word in holy places. You can find a word in the burning bush. I don't know what the word is on the street, but when you approach the holy there is a Word from God for God's people. A holy word—a word that is time tested.

- Street talk says "you are knee deep in trouble"—but God talk says trouble don't last always, for God is the only eternal reality.
- Street talk says "you are unqualified"—but God talk says please be patient with me for God is not through with me yet, for I am just like you, still being shaped.

- Street talk says "there's nothing you can do"—but God talk says if you take one step God will take two, for God expeditiously responds to those who seek deliverance.
- Street talk says "I have some bad news"—but God talk says that there is a bright side somewhere, and this is just my opportunity to simply shift or relocate to a place of promise and refuge.
- Street talk says "your family is falling apart"—but God talk says that a family that prays together stays together, just as the Father, the Son, and the Holy Spirit are one.
- Street talk says "see if you can get out of this one"—but God talk says He's a Bridge over trouble water, and God's invisible hand will carry you through and over your ordeal.
- Street talk says "it is impossible"—but God talk says the Lord will make a way somehow, for God will use the least likely person or avenue to save you.
- Street talk says "it's too late"—but God talk says He's an on time God, for God is perfect timing.
- Street talk says "Why are you still waiting on God?"—but God talk says He may not come when you want Him but He's always on time, for God's moment is not for us to determine.
- Street talk says "you are crazy"—but God talk says He's a heart fixer and mind regulator, who will change your perspective to life and ease your worried mind.
- Street talk says "I know what you use to do"—but God talk says He picked me up, turned me around and place my feet on higher ground, for I'm no longer the old self.
- Street talk says "you ain't all of that"—but God talk says ain't He alright? For although I'm nothing, God is an awesome God, God

is all together good.

O, we are on Holy Ground and if we are faithful to the burning bush down here—when the flames of life fade away there shall be another bush. There shall be a throne with seven lamps burning and blazing along with twenty-four elders and we shall sing *holy, holy, holy, is God Almighty!* Let the church say, Amen!

Appendix B
Sermon

Early Sunday Morning

Luke 24:1-3

(1) *On the first day of the week, very early in the morning, the women took*
the spices they had prepared and went to the tomb.
(2) *They found the stone rolled away from the tomb,*
(3) *but when they entered, they did not find the body of the Lord Jesus.*

Along with this text we are also reminded of the sacred utterance of
our religious experience in that this is the day that "He got up early
Sunday morning." Today we gather to commemorate and celebrate the
resurrection of Jesus as we are reminded of God's liberating love for the
downtrodden. We have gathered early this morning to observe His
overcoming of death. We do this not only at sunrise on Easter Sunday,
but each Sunday which represents a mini-Easter; we arise early in the
morning and make our way to the Lord's house. Not Saturday because
that's premature; things have yet to happen that would lead to an even
more reverent response to God—and certainly not Monday because
that's too late—the response is not necessarily a denial but a delay in
acknowledging the divine works that have been exhibited in one's life.
Besides, Monday is the day when many of us unfortunately worship
other gods. Not Saturday and not Monday but according to (kairos)

God's timing we come early Sunday morning. Believers therefore communally worship early Sunday mornings as a testament to the Lord's Day and a new first day of the week.

Our coming is both theologically inspired and biblically influenced. The text says that it was early in the morning of the first day of the week. It was early Sunday morning. This early connotes the coming into being and mysterious dawning of a new day that is not to be contributed to anyone except God. The earliness of Christ's resurrection is the bridge between death and new life. Let us consider what took place on the early morning of Jesus' resurrection and what we are still privilege to witness on Sunday mornings.

Early Sunday Morning is a time of Reverence. Women took spices that they had prepared to the tomb of Jesus. As it was custom, these women came to the sepulcher to embalm and anoint the body of their beloved Jesus. They came to scatter sweet spices upon and about the body of Jesus. They did not come expecting Jesus to do anything for them, for they assumed that He was still dead, but yet they brought oil to anoint Him. As soon as they could they made their way to the tomb to reverently honor the Lord with rather expensive oils and spices. They could not wait another minute to honor the man that loved them so they came early in the morning on the first day of the week...

Early Sunday Morning is a time of Revelation. When the women— Mary Magdalene, Joanna, Mary the mother of James, and others got there, they found the stone rolled away from the tomb. The stone that had been placed upon the tomb by the Roman rule to suggest an end to an era and to keep Jesus in and keep others from Him had been removed. An unveiling and uncovering took place early that morning. That which was concealed and kept hidden was now revealed in that God's reign was made noticeably evident in that the kingdom of God is more powerful than Caesar's kingdom. The invisible became somewhat visible in the morning. Worship is a revelatory experience. When we gather to reverence God, God reveals unto us the mysteries of life; that which we have never seen or heard. The answer that you have been longing for will be revealed. Perhaps it was early one Sunday morning when you found out that weeping may endure for the night but joy comes in the morning...

Early Sunday Morning is time of Resurrection. The text says that they entered the tomb, and found no body in it. The body of the Jesus was not in the tomb that they buried Him in. They left Him there and they knew that He was in there Friday for they were at His crucifixion and did not scatter at the hour of His burial. Perhaps they were there when Joseph of Arimathea paid for His burial plot, but now there is no body in the grave. It was early Sunday morning that those who gathered to worship Him discovered that the one who was dead is now alive. Those who stayed home missed it and had to be told and informed about it, but these women were there. No one saw Him get up, because it happened early in the morning. Jesus' early rising is experienced but not fully captured. Early Sunday morning is the genesis of a new creation; a beginning that is determined by God only. The early, suggests an invisible and unseen movement of God that did not require human influence or approval.

As recorded in the 23rd chapter they knew the exact time of His fall and death. It was the ninth hour. It was about 3pm and darkness covered the land, but all Luke could say about His resurrection is that it was early in the morning. Isn't it amazing how individuals can remember your demise, downfall or death but they can't seem to recall or for that matter, believe your date of resurrection and overcoming. Resurrection takes place when others don't expect it, primarily because they were not there and God did not need them anyhow. The late Miles Jerome Jones once said that the essence of resurrection is showing up in places where folk don't expect to see you.[115] I agree with that Prince of Preaching and would like to add that resurrection is also not being found in the places that persons dropped you off at. They buried Him, but God raised Him. They thought that He would be in the same place they left Him or last saw Him, but God moved Him, God elevated Him, God raised Him from the dead.

It is my assertion that great things happen in the early morning. Resurrection happens in the early morning. Persons are wondering where you are—they are stopping by your house right now—they are ringing your phone right now—they are awaiting a response to their text message right now—but they can't find you, because God has raised you...

And when we are raised for the last time we are reminded that everyday shall be like Sunday and Sabbath shall have no end. Which Sunday? The Sunday that He wiped away your tears; the Sunday that He lifted your burdens; the Sunday that He rolled away your enemy's stony heart; the Sunday that He healed you of your malady; the Sunday that salvation was extended to your starving soul; the Sunday that He raised you from your proverbial death; the Sunday of endless worship, perpetual praise, and eternal rest...

---

[115] This is a personal anecdotal statement made upon reflection of countless lectures and statements made by my former Homiletics instructor at the Samuel DeWitt Proctor School of Theology at Virginia Union University.

Bibliography

Augustine. *Saint Augustine On Christian Teaching*. Translated by R.P.H. Green. Oxford: Oxford University Press, 1997.

Blount, Brian K. *Cultural Interpretation: Reorienting New Testament Criticism*. Minneapolis: Fortress Press, 1995.

Burke, Kenneth. *The Rhetoric of Religion: Studies in Logology*. Berkeley: University of California Press, 1961.

Buttrick, David. *Homiletic: Moves and Structures*. Philadelphia: Fortress Press, 1987.

Cannon, Katie Geneva. *Teaching Preaching: Isaac Rufus Clark and Black Sacred Rhetoric*. New York: Continuum, 2002.

Cooper-Lewter, Nicholas, and Henry H. Mitchell. *Soul Theology: The Heart of American Black Culture*. Nashville: Abingdon Press, 1986.

Courlander, Harold. *A Treasury of African Folklore: The Oral Literature, Traditions, Myths, Legends, Epics, Tales, Recollections, Wisdom, Sayings, and Humor of Africa*. New York: Marlowe and Company, 1996.

Craddock, Fred B. *As One Without Authority*. Revised and with New Sermons. St. Louis: Chalice Press, 2001.

DuBois, W.E.B. *The Soul of Black Folk*. New York: Bantam Books, 1903.

Edwards, O.C. Jr. *A History of Preaching*. Nashville: Abingdon Press, 2004.

Equiano, Olaudah. "Traditional Ibo Religion and Culture." In *African American Religious History: A Documentary Witness*, ed. Milton C. Sernett, 13-18. Durham: Duke University Press, 1999.

Frazier, E. Franklin. "The Negro Church and Assimilation." In *African American Religious Thought: An Anthology*, ed. Cornel West and Eddie S. Glaude Jr., 62-73. Louisville: Westminster John Knox Press, 2003.

Glaude, Eddie S. Jr. "Of the Black Church and the Making of a Black Public." In *African American Religious Thought: An Anthology*, ed. Cornell West and Eddie S. Glaude, Jr., 338-365. Louisville: Westminster John Knox Press, 2003.

Harris, James H. *The Word Made Plain: The Power and Promise of Preaching.* Minneapolis: Fortress Press, 2004.

Hilkert, Mary Catherine. *Naming Grace: Preaching and the Sacramental Imagination.* New York: Continuum, 1997.

Hilkert, Mary Catherine and Robert J. Schreiter. *The Praxis of the Reign of God: An Introduction to the Theology of Edward Schillebeeckx.* With a prologue by Edward Schillebeeckx. New York: Fordham University Press, 2002.

Johnson, James Weldon and J. Rosamund Johnson. *The Book of American Negro Spirituals.* New York: The Viking Press, 1925.

Jones, Kirk Byron. *The Jazz of Preaching: How to Preach with Great Freedom and Joy.* Nashville: Abingdon Press, 2004.

Kwadwo, Osei. *An Outline of Asante History: Part 1, 3rd ed.* Kumasi: Cita Press, 2004.

Larue, Cleophus J. *The Heart of Black Preaching.* Louisville: Westminster John Knox Press, 2000.

————. "Two Ships Passing in the Night." In *What's the Matter with Preaching Today?*, ed. Mike Graves, 127-144. Louisville: Westminster John Knox Press, 2004.

Lischer, Richard. *The Preacher King: Martin Luther King Jr. and The Word that Moved America*. New York: Oxford University Press, 1995.

Mathews, Donald G. *Religion in the Old South*. Chicago: University of Chicago Press, 1977.

Mbiti, John, S. *African Religions and Philosophy: 2nd ed*. New Hampshire: Heinemann, 1990.

Mitchell, Henry H. *Black Belief: Folk Beliefs of Blacks in America and West Africa*. New York: Harper & Row, 1975.

————. *Black Preaching: The Recovery of a Powerful Art*. Nashville: Abingdon Press, 1990.

————. *Celebration and Experience in Preaching*. Nashville: Abingdon Press, 1990.

Proctor, Samuel D. *The Certain Sound of the Trumpet: Crafting a Sermon of Authority*. Valley Forge: Judson Press, 1994.

Raboteau, Albert J. *Slave Religion: The Invisible Institution in the Antebellum South*. Oxford: Oxford University Press, 1978.

Ramshaw, Gail. *Reviving Sacred Speech: The Meaning of Liturgical Language*. Akron: OSL Publications, 2000.

Resner, André Jr. *Preacher and Cross: Person and Message in Theology and Rhetoric*. Grand Rapids: William B. Eerdmans Publishing Company, 1999.

Smitherman, Geneva. *Talkin and Testifyin: The Language of Black America*. Detroit: Wayne State University Press, 1977.

Thomas, Frank A. *They Like to Never Quit Praisin' God: The Role of Celebration in Preaching.* Cleveland: Pilgrim Press, 1997.

Thurman, Howard. "The Negro Spiritual Speaks of Life and Death: Love." In *African American Religious Thought: An Anthology,* ed. Cornel West and Eddie S. Glaude Jr., 29-61. Louisville: Westminster John Knox Press, 2003.

Tisdale, Leonora Tubbs. *Preaching as Local Theology and Folk Art.* Minneapolis: Fortress Press, 1997.

Walker, Wyatt Tee. *Spirits That Dwell in Deep Woods: The Prayer and Praise Hymns of the Black Religious Experience.* Chicago: GIA Publications, 1987.

Waznak, Robert P. *An Introduction to the Homily.* Collegeville: Liturgical Press, 1998.

Webb, Joseph M. *Preaching and the Challenge of Pluralism.* St. Louis: Chalice Press, 1998.

West, Cornel. "American Africans in Conflict: Alienation in an Insecure Culture." In *African American Religious Thought: An Anthology,* ed. Cornel West and Eddie S. Glaude Jr., 77-98. Louisville: Westminster John Knox Press, 2003.

White, James F. "The Study of Protestant Worship." In *Protestant Worship: Traditions in Transition.* Louisville: Westminster/John Knox Press, 1989.

Wilmore, Gayraud S. *Black Religion and Black Radicalism: An Interpretation of the Religious History of African Americans.* 3rd ed. Revised. New York: Orbis Books, 1999.

Wisdom, Andrew Carl. *Preaching to a Multi-Generational Assembly.* Collegeville: Liturgical Press, 2004.

Index

About the Author

Dr. Gregory M. Howard is a professor of Religious Studies at Virginia Union University in Richmond, Virginia and is pastor of Union Branch Baptist Church in Chesterfield, Virginia.

Dr Howard earned his B.S. in Organizational Management and Development from Bluefield College; a Master of Divinity from the Samuel DeWitt Proctor School of Theology at Virginia Union University and his Doctor of Ministry in Preaching from Aquinas Institute of Theology in St. Louis, Missouri.

Other Titles from BorderStone Press, LLC
www.borderstonepress.com

Michael A.G Haykin $19.95
The Empire of the Holy Spirit
ISBN #: 978-0-9842284-7-8

Terry L. Wilder, editor $14.95
The Lost Sermons of Scottish Baptist Peter Grant
ISBN #: 978-0-9842284-9-2

G.K. Chesterton $14.95
The Man who was Thursday
a Nightmare
ISBN #: 978-0-9842284-1-6

Moses Maimonides $14.95
Eight Chapters on Ethics
ISBN #: 978-0-9842284-2-3

Dale E. Palmer $14.95
Stones from the Brook
A Treasury of Godly Reflections from Life's Journey
ISBN #: 978-0-9842284-6-1

Joshua F. Drake $14.95
Recovering Music Education as a Christian Liberal Art
ISBN #: 978-0-9842284-4-7

Edward Tuckerman Potter $14.95
Bible Stories for Children in Bible Language
ISBN #: 978-0-9842284-0-9

Brian R. Mooney, editor $14.95
Holy Communion and the Bible
from the 1928 Book of Common Prayer
ISBN #: 978-0-9842284-8-5

*All orders subject to applicable sales tax and shipping rates. Prices are listed in U.S. dollars and subject to conversion and applicable taxes for all international orders. Wholesale pricing is available upon request. For pricing and availability please contact orders@borderstonepress.com